Praise for *How to Make the Most of Every Media Appearance*

"The well-prepared interviewer can control the focus and content of an interview with an ill-prepared interviewee. On the other hand, the well-prepared interviewee can always get his or her message across, no matter how skilled the interviewer. George Merlis's fine book details how to meet the media and prevail."

—David Hartman, original host,
"Good Morning America"

"Be prepared! George Merlis's book calls upon both interviewers and interview subjects alike to adopt the Boy Scouts motto. The interviewer has prepared for your dialog by knowing everything about you in advance, so you'd better be prepared to have all the answers in order to successfully handle any media appearance. Merlis's book is the most valuable tool for any media situation."

—Robin Leach, celebrity TV journalist

"Being media savvy is an essential survival skill in the twenty-first century. I am constantly amazed at the smart, successful people who stumble and stammer when a camera is pointed in their face. George Merlis's book will help media neophytes become media pros."

—Leonard Maltin, film critic and historian

"Written concisely, expertly, entertainingly, and—above all else—helpfully, George Merlis's book reveals the secrets and intricacies of what goes into a good interview and builds up the reader's confidence to plunge into the electronic arena. The result? Even I'm ready for my close-up, Mr. DeMille."

—Stephen M. Silverman, editor, People.com News Daily

"George Merlis knows everything about blasting through the background sound and making your point. He is not just a great coach for acing a media interview—his rules work for all of life. You can use them on TV, at meetings, on job interviews, on dates, or ordering a pizza by phone! He's talking about being the most effective you."

—Diane Sawyer, ABC News

"George Merlis is one of the best TV producers in the business. He wrote this book in self-defense. He's spent his career locked in editing rooms all over the world trying to help people sound intelligent and make their points. And he's tired. Help him out, read this book. And if I'll be interviewing you at any time in the next five years, please, read this book."

—Joel Siegel, film critic and entertainment editor, "Good Morning America"

"George Merlis's book is a must for anybody facing an interview situation. It even helps those of us asking the questions."

—Bob Goen, co-host, "Entertainment Tonight"

HOW TO MAKE THE MOST OF EVERY MEDIA APPEARANCE

GETTING YOUR MESSAGE ACROSS ON THE AIR, IN PRINT, OR ONLINE

GEORGE MERLIS

McGraw·Hill

New York   Chicago   San Francisco   Lisbon   London   Madrid   Mexico City
Milan   New Delhi   San Juan   Seoul   Singapore   Sydney   Toronto

The *McGraw·Hill* Companies

Library of Congress Cataloging-in-Publication Data

Merlis, George, 1940–
    How to make the most of every media appearance : getting your message across on
the air, in print, or online / George Merlis.
        p.   cm.
    Includes index.
    ISBN 0-07-141671-4
    1. Interviewing on television.   2. Interviewing in journalism.   I. Title.

PN1992.8.I68M47 2003
    158′.39—dc21   2003051338

1 2 3 4 5 6 7 8 9 0   AGM/AGM   2 1 0 9 8 7 6 5 4 3

ISBN 0-07-141671-4

Interior design by Hespenheide Design

McGraw-Hill books are available at special quantity discounts to use as premiums and sales
promotions, or for use in corporate training programs. For more information, please write to the
Director of Special Sales, Professional Publishing, McGraw-Hill, Two Penn Plaza, New York, NY
10121-2298. Or contact your local bookstore.

This book is printed on acid-free paper.

CONTENTS

CHAPTER 1

MEET AND MASTER THE MEDIA

"In the future everyone will be world-famous for fifteen minutes."
                                                    —ANDY WARHOL, 1968

With the mass media's insatiable appetite growing in a geometric progression, Andy Warhol's 1968 prediction is looking like tomorrow's naive understatement. Are *you* prepared for *your* fifteen minutes? What about the altogether likely possibility that your fifteen minutes will stretch into fifteen hours, fifteen days, or fifteen weeks of media attention? You have two basic choices in any interview: willingly comply with a reporter's agenda (which may or may not match your own) or take control and work your agenda. The difference between compliance and mastery is the set of skills and body of knowledge presented in this book. In these pages I've used everything I've learned in my forty-year-long print and broadcast career to help you master your media encounters. That career has encompassed a lot of interviews. I have conducted or overseen ten thousand print or broadcast interviews or television appearances in my years as a reporter, an editor, and a producer. They have run the gamut from friendly chats on "Good Morning America" to tough, adversarial confrontations on investigative TV newsmagazines. I've interviewed a vast number of individuals myself, and I've researched, produced, and written major stories—including exposés—for newspapers, magazines, and television networks. For close to twenty years, I've also media-trained spokespersons. My clients have ranged from rocket scientists to rock stars!

The skills I teach when I media-train people like yourself are based on my observations and practices honed during a full career as reporter, writer, editor, television news producer, and media-training consultant. If you are ever interviewed by the media—if you face even a remote prospect of being interviewed—this book will supply you with a storehouse of vital information. The skills require some practice and repetition because some of them—like transitioning from the reporter's question to your answer—are counterintuitive to many people. The biggest mistake you can make is to treat an interview like a conversation. It is not, no matter how skillful the reporter is in appearing casual and off-the-cuff. An interview is work, for both the reporter and you. He has a job to do—to get information for his story. You have a job, too—to be sure that the information he gets from you is the information you want him to get, and only that information.

There are basic skills, such as speaking in soundbites, illustrating your key points with word pictures, and keeping your answers short, simple, and comprehensible, that you should acquire whether you are preparing for an appearance on a national investigative broadcast magazine like "60 Minutes," you have been booked for a product-plugging opportunity on a local radio show, or you are facing an in-depth interview by a well-prepared reporter for a newspaper like the *Washington Post* or the *New York Times*. Anyone who might one day be called upon to be interviewed for the defense of a point of view or to promote a project or product in any medium needs to learn how to speak to the media the way the media speak to us, how to give answers to a reporter's questions, and how to parry his catalog of dirty tricks—all of which and more are covered in this book. These skills include how to create your own agenda for an interview, how to work that agenda into the interview, how to protect yourself in a hostile or uninformed interview, and how to reach beyond the reporter to convey your message to his viewers, readers, or listeners.

Whether you are to be questioned for *Newsweek*, "CBS Evening News," or the local weekly newspaper, that interview is your best opportunity to reach a wide audience with a message. This book will tell you how to formulate your message and how to work it gracefully and effectively into your interview. Preparation is the key; it can help anyone do more than merely survive a media encounter. In fact, the easily learned set of skills presented in this book can help anyone quite literally master the media.

I have designed this book to be a simple step-by-step how-to guide. Whenever possible I've illustrated my points with anecdotes or case histories that serve as object lessons. In addition, this book has an interactive component. Periodically I'm going to ask you to do a little homework, to fill out some worksheets in preparation for an interview. These exercises are very important because they will teach you how to get ready for the real thing. After preparing correctly for your interview, you will feel confident about facing a reporter, whether that questioner is a fawning fan or an aggressive inquisitor. You'll get the most out of the book if you avail yourself of these interactive opportunities. Additional copies of all worksheets in this book may be downloaded from www.master-the-media.com.

A word about how this book is organized: we'll begin by exploring the basic media-mastery skills you'll need whether you're being interviewed by someone representing a newspaper, a magazine, a company newsletter, or a local or national television program. These are fundamental communication skills like speaking in complete sentences, beginning your answers with a topic sentence or a verbal headline, and being quoteworthy. You will need to master these skills in order to be a successful interview subject. Then we'll move on to television's unique and specific demands, the little tricks of the trade that make you a good guest or an interesting interview, like speaking with animation, illustrating your points with gestures, and engaging your interviewer. These television skills are largely matters of style and cosmetics that in no way substitute for content but rather are designed to enhance the substance of what you are saying. Good television style—making yourself an interesting TV speaker—is no different from good writing style. The style makes the message more palatable and comprehensible. As a television viewer you already know this. If you are presented with a bad interview subject, your attention will wander and you will absorb little. Watch a good interview subject, and your attention remains focused and you take away her principal message points. You will recognize the interview subject the next time she is on television, and you look forward to what she has to say. She informs in an entertaining, engrossing way.

Increasingly, television spokespersons are being asked to demonstrate rather than merely talk. Television programs want show-and-tell these days. If you're talking about a new electronic device, you'd best be prepared to demonstrate it. If you're discussing a medical breakthrough, television prefers that you be able to illustrate it by bringing images and that you be able to narrate over those images. The tricks of this aspect of the spokesperson's trade, which you'll discover in greater detail later in the book, include knowing how to show objects to the camera, knowing how to move on camera, and knowing how to talk about your subject while demonstrating or illustrating it.

The book also includes specific information on radio interviews, news conferences, and interviews conducted over the phone. In the case of radio, you must rely totally on your voice for communication. You'll learn how to energize your voice, how to make your points more concise, and how to be sure the audience knows who is speaking. As far as news conferences are concerned, facing fifteen reporters is not fifteen times more challenging than facing a single reporter; you'll learn why that is true. In fact, it is possible to use the large group to your advantage by focusing your attention on those reporters most likely to treat you and your point of view fairly. And the telephone offers us both risks and opportunities; you'll learn how to avoid the first and take advantage of the second. You'll see how you can capitalize on the fact that your interviewer can't see what you're doing so he'll never know if you've got lots of helpful material right in front of you to aid you in getting your agenda into the interview.

I suggest you read the entire book and complete all the exercises long before your first interview. There is a lot of material to absorb in this book, and cramming just before the "exam" doesn't work when you're prepping for a media interview any more than it did when you pulled an all-nighter in college. Moreover, you need time to process your agenda for each specific interview, and you don't want that process compromised by speed-reading.

How the Media Use Interviews

Before creating any agendas, you should understand just how important an interview is in the construction of a news story. Interviews, whether used as a source for verbatim quotes or just for editorial background and research guidance, are the very basis for most of the news stories we read and see. The print media initially perfected the practice of using the interview as a key building block of a story, and the technique was adapted by the broadcast media to meet their unique needs.

The Print Media

Print journalists create stories by interviewing a source or a number of sources and then paraphrasing or directly quoting what the sources said. The writers combine these quotes and paraphrases with other material, including firsthand observations by the journalist or a colleague, press releases, earlier articles, and research from books and the Web. Then they craft a narrative from all the combined source material.

Sometimes the story is from a single point of view, as in "The administration is introducing measures to ensure that the National Oceanic and Atmospheric Administration (NOAA) has sufficient research funds to thoroughly examine climate change." At other times, the story comes from multiple points of view, as in "The administration is introducing measures to ensure that the National Oceanic and Atmospheric Administration (NOAA) has sufficient research funds to thoroughly examine climate change; however, congressional sources say that a substantial number of House members and a few senators don't believe there is any climate change and will oppose authorizations to study the matter." Either way, the story will use quotes and paraphrases from various spokespeople to flesh out the account.

Another type of article, the Q&A, is basically just that: questions asked by a reporter and the interview subject's answers in direct quotes. It is the nearest thing in the print media to a live broadcast interview. The only editing that occurs in one of these articles is the condensation of some answers and the elimination of whole questions and answers that, in the reporter's opinion, don't further the flow.

The Broadcast Media

Television stories are created by splicing together three basic elements: interviews or direct quotes, on-camera or voice-over transitions by the correspondent, and voice-over narration of footage that illustrates elements of the story, which is called B-roll. Much of the correspondent's on-camera and voice-over material will be created by paraphrasing spokespersons' quotations garnered in interviews. The rest will come from the same sorts of sources the print reporter used. Radio stories are similarly structured, except that they eliminate the B-roll and instead include bits of so-called actuality audio, or nonspeaking sound recorded on the scene of the news story. Actuality audio might include the sound of trees being cut down for a story on shrinking rain forests or the sound of cars' motors and horns for a story on traffic congestion.

The following is an example of how television might report the hypothetical NOAA budget story cited earlier. Notice how the interview is a key ingredient in the edited news story.

Correspondent on camera in front of the White House: "The administration, concerned about climate change and global warning, is seeking a supplemental appropriation from Congress to fund research by the National Oceanic and Atmospheric Administration, or NOAA, into the causes of the phenomenon."

Next, over footage of an earth-orbiting weather satellite, the correspondent's voice is heard (this is his voice-over): "The White House feels that two more satellites like this one are needed to adequately survey the situation." Then comes a soundbite from the presidential press secretary or science adviser expressing concern about ramifications of climate change on agriculture and commerce. This is followed by B-roll of the Capitol building and a voice-over narration by the correspondent: "However, on Capitol Hill, the announcement was greeted with skepticism." Cut to an on-camera soundbite by Representative Rupkins: "My district hasn't seen any climate change, and I'm not going to allow this administration boondoggle to get to the floor because it's a waste of taxpayer dollars." This might be followed by a rebuttal soundbite from the White House spokesperson because conflict makes for good TV.

Live Broadcast Interviews

Whether they are broadcast on radio or television, live interviews are segments in which a host interviews a subject for a specific length of time (usually with breaks only for commercials) and, in some cases, invites viewer or listener call-in questions. The interview may be long or short. For example, my alma mater, "Good Morning America," and the other morning programs used to schedule interviews to run at least five minutes to as long as eight minutes. Today, those morning show interviews have been whittled down to three to five minutes because a generation of viewers reared watching MTV and thirty-second commercials has learned to absorb information in very brief bursts. In fact, many viewers won't tolerate longer interviews; their attention begins to wander if the subject, venue, and tone aren't changed quickly and often. It might be said that we have a nation suffering from attention deficit disorder. Or perhaps we've learned how to quickly grasp and process a rapid-fire flow of information. Whether that's a curse or a blessing we'll have to leave to the social scientists and psychologists. For our purposes it's sufficient to know that the short form interview is a fact of broadcast life today and spokespersons must learn to communicate concisely.

Of course, there remain broadcasts (like PBS's "Charlie Rose Show") that will sometimes give over an entire hour to a single guest. And a PBS hour is almost an hour—between fifty-six and fifty-eight minutes—as opposed to a commercial broadcast hour, which generally runs only forty-four minutes once the commercial breaks are factored in. I place the "Rose" show in the live category even though it is taped because it is "live to tape." That is, it is most often taped in real time, without stopping and with minimal, if any, editing.

Whatever the length, a live or live-to-tape interview gives you the most control, since it goes out to the audience unedited. The opportunity is there, but so is the challenge. There is no second chance in a live interview, no calling up after the fact and saying, "There's something else you should know. . . ." So it's incumbent on you to get it right the first time. The skills you learn in these pages will help you to do that.

The key to media mastery is learning how to be interviewed. This book will prove to be your bible for media encounters. To that end, let's begin with the five commandments of interviews.

The Five Commandments of Interviews

1. Thou shalt be prepared.
2. Thou shalt know to whom thou art speaking.
3. Thou shalt be quoteworthy.
4. Thou shalt practice, practice, practice.
5. Thou shalt not lie, evade, nor cop an attitude.

These five commandments should become your mantra before any media appearance. They will be discussed in more detail in the next two chapters. Keep them foremost in your mind and put them into practice, and you will be assured of a successful appearance.

It has been said that fear of public speaking appearances tops even fear of death for most people. And how much more public can an appearance be than a news media interview? That fear business may be a convenient myth concocted by public speaking coaches. But the fact of the matter is we may have to appear in public numerous times and we only die once. So whether the fear of an interview or speech is greater than, on a par with, or even less than the fear of dying, it certainly is a more frequently encountered dread. It is quite likely that the root cause of both fears is the feeling that in these situations we exercise little or no control. That's where this book comes in—at least in the public appearance sphere. It will help you overcome the fear of interviews and other public appearances by giving you the tools to take control of the situation. When you get through these pages and you begin to use the preinterview worksheets, you'll lose your fear and you'll view media exposure as an opportunity, not as a threat. The skill set you will learn here will level the media playing field and may even tilt it in your favor. Let's begin our journey to media mastery with the most essential fundamental: preparation. In the next chapter you'll learn how to prepare for any interview.

CHAPTER 2

THE BOY SCOUT COMMANDMENTS

Over the years I've observed that the most successful interview subjects are men and women who, regardless of what they're speaking about, approach their media encounters with a sense of purpose, a positive—even eager—attitude, and an enthusiasm for their subject. For some outgoing and passionately committed people this approach comes naturally. For others it is learned behavior. While I may appear to be describing the ideal television guest, you should bear in mind that the reporter interviewing you for the local newspaper is—like the television viewer—an audience, too. If you can engage a hundred thousand or a million people in a television appearance, you ought to be able to use the same skills and attitude to engage that reporter, your audience of one. Successful interview subjects consciously or unconsciously heed a certain interview discipline. To embrace that discipline, you'll need to learn and obey the five commandments of interviews.

If the term *commandments* seems a little strong, that's intentional. You don't want to leave your interview results to chance, so you need to play by a strict set of rules. The most effective spokespersons are those who are single-minded in their dedication to expressing their message in a way that is simultaneously entertaining, comprehensive, and comprehensible. To become that messenger requires a certain level of dedication, which can easily be mastered by those who follow the commandments. The first two are called the Boy Scout commandments because they take their inspiration from the Scouts' famous motto, Be Prepared.

Let me tell you about two of my own experiences as an interview subject: one when I was prepared, the other when I was not. The first time I was ever interviewed by a newspaper reporter was in 1960. The reporter who interviewed me was Ed Klein, who, at the time of the interview, was working for the now-defunct *New York World-Telegram and Sun*. Ed was questioning me because I had recently been arrested, interrogated, and expelled from the Soviet Union for, in the words of a Soviet police document, forcing "noxious propaganda" on supposedly unwilling Moscow citizens. (Actually, the Moscow citizens had been clamoring for copies of a State Department exchange magazine called *Amerika*.) Ed wrote a long, complete story filled with direct quotes. It was, as they say in the newspaper trade, a good yarn: American college kid caught up in the East-West confrontation and tossed out of the country in an exhibition of bureaucratic fumbling worthy of the Keystone Kops. I was very pleased with the piece; it accurately reflected what I said, mostly by using my own words to tell the story.

I went on to become a newspaper reporter (at the very same *New York World-Telegram and Sun*) and then a television producer. About ten years passed before I myself was again an interview subject. By this point, I had conducted hundreds of interviews.

Given my career as a journalist, I thought that I knew how to be interviewed and that it was going to be easy. The journalist interviewing me was only looking for a few comments on a benign situation at ABC, where I worked. This interview was conducted over the phone by a columnist I had known for several years, and I did not feel intimidated in the least. In fact, I was totally at ease during the interview; our conversation was brief, friendly, and casual. And yet the next day, when I read the few paragraphs the columnist had written about the situation, I found them to be oddly unsatisfying. There were no direct quotes; what I had said was paraphrased.

Apparently, I had failed to express myself in a quoteworthy manner—nothing I'd said warranted a direct quote. I had been neither concise nor specific enough to earn the medal of quotation marks around my own words. That seemed strange to me because as a reporter I was always on the lookout for that good quote for my own stories. Ten years earlier, talking to Ed Klein, I had given a lot of good quotes. Looking back on the experience, I suppose I had been entertaining as well as informative in that first interview; I had helped the reporter with that good yarn. The second time around, I contributed nothing beyond basic, factual answers. I made no effort to excite or entertain the reader; I was, sin of all sins, dull! I could—and should—have illustrated my answers with wit, with anecdotes, with engaging metaphors. Instead, I just answered the questions as if I had been on the stand in a court-room—offering barely more than "yes" and "no" responses.

Certainly, I had answered the second interviewer's questions factu-ally—indeed, the facts were there, but the story just sat on the page, drab as a dirty, old, limp mop. It wasn't his fault; he'd done what he could with what I'd given him. I just hadn't given him much to work with. Which just goes to show that while you may be a master at your trade, you may not be a master at all trades—especially if you don't pos-sess the proper tools or training. This story leads us to our first commandment.

Commandment 1: Thou Shalt Be Prepared

What was the difference between the two interviews? In the first, I had a story to tell, an adventure to relate—my arrest and interrogation by the Soviet police, my expulsion from the country, my hero's welcome in Communist Poland where, despite the shared ideology, anything that smacked of anti-Soviet or anti-Russian behavior was warmly greeted. Also, I had an agenda to serve: I felt my adventure dramatically illus-trated the freedom-smothering effect of life in a totalitarian police state. In the second interview, I'd been a passive and not at all creative par-ticipant with no real story of my own to relate. I had no agenda to press in the second interview; I had no message to get out to the columnist's readers. I merely serviced his agenda, which was to learn a few facts about an ongoing situation at ABC News. And I served that agenda of his rather poorly by not being very quotable. Had I known then what I know now, I would have used the opportunity of that interview to advance a new documentary series ABC News was about to launch. But the columnist wasn't asking about that, and, slavishly serving only his agenda, I did not even consider working a mention of the series into my answers. It was a classic missed opportunity.

In the spirit of "do as I say, not as I did," remember this: every time you are interviewed, you should have a prepared story, a point of view, a message or series of messages. An interview is an opportunity, and to go into an interview unprepared, without an agenda of your own, is to totally blow that opportunity. Unless you are a movie star or a public official, those opportunities don't arrive every day. In fact, for many of us, interviews are so rare that we might consider each one a once-in-a-lifetime opportunity. If you know an interview is coming, prepare. In my case, it wasn't as if the columnist had sidled up to me at the local ABC watering hole and casually inquired, "What's new?" No, he had called me up, told me he was working on a story, and asked me if he could get some information from me. I even had to call him back, so there had been some prep time—which I did not use to my advantage. I blew the opportunity. But that was the last time I ever made that mistake.

An Interview as Performance

In the first chapter, I noted that I've done media training for every sort of profession from rocket scientist to rock star. When I am dealing with the rock stars, I always tell them to think of an interview as a performance. Folks who are more Joe Everybody than Joe Cocker can do the same.

I challenge those entertainers with this thought: "You wouldn't get up on a stage and begin singing without knowing what you're going to sing, would you? You know your music, your lyrics, your instrumentation, and your choreography. You rehearse your material." The same holds true, I tell them, for an interview. They need to know and rehearse their material, and then they need to perform it. Entertainment clients understand that right away. For people in the sciences, the business world, government, and public service, the idea of an interview as a performance may seem a little strange at first. But once they accept the notion that communicating effectively requires performing skills, it's pretty easy to get them to appreciate the need for knowing their "lyrics," polishing their techniques, and rehearsing their steps.

Obviously, I am not suggesting that rocket scientists—or anyone else, for that matter—sing and dance for reporters. But to make the most of any media opportunity, they—and you—need to have an agenda that's ready to be performed. In other words, Thou shalt be prepared.

Intentional Message Statements

The first step in fulfilling that preparedness commandment is to formulate an agenda. That agenda should be composed of what I call intentional message statements (IMSs). These are the points you feel must be made during the interview. I use the word *intentional* because these are the message statements you plan on expressing, not inadvertent points that happen to have a positive impact on your agenda. Not every message you deliver must wear a big, verbal happy face. Your IMSs could be an effective health warning, an attack on a political foe's policies, or some other bit of crucial, but downbeat, information. For example, I saw a public health official interviewed on one of the cable news channels the other day. He was talking about the fact that every year in America, influenza kills more people than AIDS. This was far from that verbal happy face, but for his purposes it was a "positive" message statement because his agenda was to persuade more people in the highest risk group—the elderly and those with compromised immune systems—to get an annual flu vaccination.

Now if you're going to obey that first commandment, Thou shalt be prepared, you cannot leave your IMSs to chance. Instead, after giving serious consideration as to exactly what your messages are, you should write them down ahead of time. Make a list and outdo Santa Claus by checking it more than twice. If you're wondering how big a list to make, I tell my clients to never go into an interview without at least five IMSs. The Appendix includes a worksheet for developing good IMSs, or, if you prefer, you can develop your own worksheets or you can download them from master-the-media.com and then write up your IMSs on your computer, where it's a lot easier to make changes or even start all over. Regardless of how you do it, before every interview, fill out a new worksheet. In doing this, you'll find that your message statements evolve, develop, and grow as you do more interviews. So going through the step of writing out your IMSs anew each and every time is not an exercise in repetition; rather, it is an aid to evolving and polishing them. But wait! Before you craft your IMSs, you need to pay heed to the second commandment.

Commandment 2: Thou Shalt Know to Whom Thou Art Speaking

This second Boy Scout, or preparedness, commandment probably has you asking yourself whether or not I'm kidding. How stupefyingly simple is this? You're talking to a reporter. Maybe it's a reporter for *Business Week*. Perhaps it's the writer-editor-publisher of your local neighborhood weekly. It could be the understanding and appealing Katie Couric on "The Today Show." Or maybe it's the deep-voiced reporter for the local all-news radio station. In each case, you're talking to an interviewer, right?

Wrong! You are never talking to an interviewer or a reporter; instead, you are talking *through* the reporter, to his readers, viewers, or listeners. It's important to plant that fact firmly in your mind before crafting your IMSs because the reporter is likely to be better informed and more knowledgeable about and more interested in what you have to say than his audience is. In fact, some reporters, especially on science, political, and technology beats, like to show off their knowledge, which may well lull you into communicating at a level that's out of reach of your real audience: the readers, viewers, and listeners.

During my seven years at "Good Morning America," the show was controlled by the ABC-TV Entertainment Division. In the early days of the show, the News Division registered loud and anguished complaints about Entertainment Division employees doing interviews with newsmakers such as politicians and statesmen. The Entertainment Division yielded to the News Division, and we were ordered to include news correspondents in any of our interviews that could be construed as newsmaking. My biggest gripe about including the correspondents was that the journalists almost always talked to the politicians and diplomats we booked on the presumption of an equal footing of knowledge with their audience, assuming that because they, the reporters, knew the inside stuff, the viewers did, too, which was not always the case. I can't tell you how many times I ground my teeth and rolled my eyes in frustration when a news correspondent would launch into a complex question about the intricacies of UN resolution 242, for example, without explaining to the viewers what resolution 242 was. The guest diplomats were only too happy to reply in equally inaccessible terms, and it inevitably fell to our "civilian" host, David Hartman, to waste valuable airtime backing up and filling in the blanks in the viewer's knowledge.

Hartman had been an actor and never attended journalism school, but he was an instinctive interviewer. One of his greatest strengths was his gift for asking questions viewers wanted answered. David never asked questions designed to show off how much he knew. While some belittled his common-man touch, audiences responded in droves, and within a year of its creation, the upstart "Good Morning America" was soundly trouncing the well-established "Today Show." That trouncing continued for more than a decade until "Today" acquired a production staff and cast who understood that viewers wanted information in language they could easily understand, not show-offs.

Identifying Your Audience and Your Interviewer's Agenda

How do you go about tailoring your messages in tone and language for your interviewer's audience? First you need to determine who that audience is. That's the easiest part of this second preparedness commandment.

All you have to do is read the publication, listen to the radio station, or watch the television program that is going to interview you, and you'll be able to determine to whom it is geared. After all, you'll want to speak differently to a reader of *Aviation Week* or *Barron's* than you will to the more general audience watching "Good Morning America" or reading *USA Today*. Your first job is to analyze who the outlet appeals to and to gauge how it appeals. In other words, does it appeal to a mass audience by shocking or frightening them? Or does it appeal to the same audience by entertaining them? Does it seek out an audience of sophisticated experts and engage them by offering detailed and solid information? Or is it a purveyor of general information for a mass audience?

If at all possible, watch, listen to, or read the work of the particular reporter who is scheduled to interview you, and take comprehensive notes on your observations. If it's going to be a print interview, read any bylined pieces so you have an idea of whether she comes to the job with a specific attitude or special knowledge. If it's a broadcast, see what tone he adopts with his interview subjects—is he friendly and cooperative or challenging and prosecutorial? In broadcasting particularly, you can't change the reporter's manner, but you should be prepared so his attitude doesn't surprise you on camera. Mike Wallace, that bulldog of a "60 Minutes" reporter, was a guest on CBS News's "The Early Show" in January 2003. Harry Smith asked him why, knowing his reputation for dogged questioning, people with something to hide submitted to his interviews. It was a good question because anyone who's watched even a modicum of television over the last thirty years knows who Wallace is and what he does in an interview. Wallace answered, "I don't know. Maybe the bad guys don't think they're really in the fraternity until they've been exposed on '60 Minutes.'"

While Mike Wallace is nationally known and his interview tactics are no secret, other interviews may require you to do more homework. You should make every effort to familiarize yourself with the interviewer's work. If your interviewer is someone who's free to express opinions—like a columnist—try to gauge her position vis-à-vis your messages. Does the reporter, the publication, or the broadcast have a point of view? Is the outlet looking for facts or for fun? Is it accurate and factual or sensational? By doing your research, you will know as much as possible and you'll be able to avoid surprises.

Speaking of surprises, I can recall a stunning example from the early days of "Good Morning America." Back then, we staged a daily six- or seven-minute debate that we called "Face Off." We would select a hot topic and, with David Hartman moderating, we would have representatives of opposing points of view argue about it. The goal was to shed some light, and maybe a little heat, on a subject that viewers would find important. One such "Face Off" featured Ron Kovic, the Marine Corps

Vietnam veteran who had been paralyzed in combat and had written about the experience in the extraordinary and passionate antiwar book *Born on the Fourth of July*. The subject was government truthfulness, or lack of truthfulness, during times of war. Kovic's adversary was retired general William Westmoreland, former commander of U.S. forces in Vietnam. Normally on "Good Morning America" we prein-terviewed our guests. For "Face Offs" these preinterviews were essen-tial lest we find out on the air that the guests agreed with each other. (That had happened only once, and we called that segment a "Face On.") General Westmoreland did not make himself available for the preinterview, but we knew he and Kovic disagreed, so we weren't par-ticularly worried about the possibility of staging another "Face On." In addition to the general's not submitting to a preinterview, I had the impression that he had not read Kovic's book and—hard as it is to believe—he did not know that this wheelchair-bound, long-haired man was a furious antiwar activist. I believe the general thought he was sit-ting down to a gentlemanly discussion, so he was totally unprepared for the articulate and passionate attack Kovic launched. The surprised gen-eral was left almost speechless by the encounter. He seemed stunned. It was all very one-sided, and a viewer need not have agreed with General Westmoreland to have felt it was a less-than-satisfying encounter. Just a little preparation would have enabled the general to put up his guard and get in his points. But he was unprepared, and Kovic pummeled him like a heavyweight pro taking on a lightweight amateur.

How Are Stories Built?

In addition to gauging the attitude of your interviewer when you are reviewing the publication or broadcast that will interview you, pay spe-cial attention to how quotes are used. For print media, does the publi-cation write stories by stringing together quotes with little interpretive continuity from the writer? Or is it largely writer opinion and obser-vation illustrated by an occasional, brief quote? In electronic media, do the soundbites run short or long? An analytical viewing will show you that the half-hour network newscasts run very short soundbites, while the magazine shows like "20/20" or "Dateline NBC" run much longer soundbites. If you know their style, you can craft your answers so they get maximum play.

When you do this you are helping yourself, by tailoring your responses to what is most likely to be used, and you are helping the reporter, by enabling him to use your direct quotes and reducing his need to paraphrase you. If the publication or broadcast uses extensive, technically detailed quotes, providing that detail in your answers helps the reporter accurately craft his story. Likewise, if the outlet goes for the common touch and you express yourself accordingly, the reporter is more likely to use your direct quotes and not have to work as hard to simplify what you said. Remember, the more a reporter is forced to paraphrase you, the more opportunity there is for your points to lose focus in the transition. Even the most sympathetic reporter filters your ideas through his perceptions and experiences when he is forced to paraphrase you. Meanings can be altered, even unintentionally, through that filtering process.

Crafting Your Message for Your Audience

Once you have identified your audience and your interviewer's likely agenda, then you're ready to craft your message. Think of what you want that audience to know about your program, company, idea, or product, and then write out the messages you want people to take away. Use IMS worksheet 1 in the appendix (or download it from www.master-the-media.com) to get started.

When you've finished with the worksheet, take as much time as you need to read your message statements aloud at least twice and think about them with as much detachment as you can muster. They are, after all, your intentional message statements. They were crafted in your self-interest. But you want your audience to be receptive to them. So the first question to ask yourself is, "Do they sound like someone speaking or do they sound too literary?" If they sound too literary, you're probably writing not for the tongue but for the eye. That is, you're writing something that is more easily absorbed when it is read than when it is spoken. While such a message can pass muster with print media, it may sound peculiar, even artificial, when heard by a television or radio audience. You should try to make your IMSs appropriate for all media, so you're best off crafting them in a more tongue-friendly way. What works for broadcasting will usually work in print, but what works in print frequently does not work for broadcast. You want to recraft your IMSs so that they are more conversational.

The second question to ask yourself is, "Do they sound like commercials or sermons?" If either is the case, that's probably because you wrote your statements exclusively from your own point of view. Instead, you should adopt the point of view of your ultimate audience. To identify with that audience, think of a single radio station whose call letters are WSIC. Whether watching your interview on TV, reading an account of it in a magazine, or listening to you on the radio, your ultimate audience is made up of people with at least this one thing in common: they are all listening to WSIC. Whether your audience is the broad-based readership of *USA Today* or the sophisticated scientists who subscribe to the magazine *Science*, they are all listening to WSIC. The call letters stand for **Why Should I Care?**

All the people you are trying to reach with your messages are subconsciously wondering why those IMSs should concern them and how your messages affect them. Remember what I said earlier about David Hartman's seizing the morning ratings lead by asking the questions viewers wanted answered? Well, that works both ways—for the interviewee as well as the interviewer. You won't always be fortunate enough to have a David Hartman–like interviewer, one who is seeking information for his viewers. Sometimes you'll be interviewed by a reporter who is too rushed, too overwhelmed, too indifferent, too expert, or too egotistical to care about the audience. So it's incumbent on you to care. You need to be careful not to craft your messages solely from your point of view. Instead, you need to broaden them so your real audience understands why it should care about them.

Earlier, I wrote about the interview with the public health official who spoke about influenza killing more people each year than AIDS. In a case like this it's pretty self-evident why a listener or reader should care. The information is a matter of life or death. But the challenge is much greater when you are trying to make people care about a message that doesn't concern a life-or-death issue. How do you make them care if you're the spokesperson for a rock band or an orbiting telescope? What if you're being interviewed to promote a new candy bar or soft drink? You need to step outside your spokesperson's role and ask yourself what it is about your messages that would interest you if you weren't the spokesperson. What about your messages would interest your Aunt Matilda and Uncle Joe? There's always something; your job now is to find it. People respond to a good story, to being entertained, to the opportunity to pursue pleasure and avoid the unpleasant. Not life-or-death like the flu, but reason enough to absorb and remember your messages. It is your job to make those connections.

Use worksheet 2 in the appendix to rework and fine-tune your IMSs for the listeners of WSIC. When you're finished, reread your IMSs aloud again and then write down specifically how you've answered the WSIC question, as I've done in the completed fictional worksheet in the appendix. Your WSIC response can be just a word or two—"entertaining," "saves money," "promotes education," "stimulates the imagination," and so on. You should have one of these WSIC responses for every one of your message statements.

Additional Tips for Successful Preparation

Commandments 1 and 2, Thou shalt be prepared and Thou shalt know to whom thou art speaking, are the most important rules for becoming a successful interview subject. Knowing before the interview begins what you want to say and to whom you'll be saying it is more than half the preparation battle. While those two commandments are the top of the "be prepared" list, there are additional preparatory steps that are no less vital in helping you be the best-prepared, most elegant and effective interview subject you can be. These steps are:

Be informed.
Eat something.
Arrive early.
Warm up.

Be discreet.

Don't assume you have friends in the media.

Be Informed

As close to the time of your interview as possible, read a newspaper and listen to a radio newscast. Even better, if you have access to the Internet, visit one of these sites: nytimes.com, cnn.com, or http://customwire.ap.org/specials/bluepage.html. Of the URLs I've listed, the last one, an Associated Press site, may prove to be the best and easiest to use. It is constantly updated with dispatches from around the globe fed in by the wire service's many reporters as well as by member news organizations. However, using it takes a few steps. The first Web page you come to features a map of the United States. Just click on any state on the map and then click on any publication or broadcast station—they all lead to the same page. That page has top news down the center and a left-side navigation bar offering you instant access to the latest news in a variety of categories: Top Stories, U.S., World, Business, Technology, Sports, Entertainment, Health, Politics, Weather. There is even an "Offbeat" category. If you're rushed, you can click on the areas you're most likely to be asked about and read up on the latest developments before going into your interview. You want to have the latest news at your fingertips before you're interviewed. You don't want to learn from the reporter that your company has just declared bankruptcy. In print, your reaction can be embarrassing: "Mr. Smith was stunned to hear from a reporter that Ynot Industries had declared bankruptcy." On camera, your dropped-jaw, stunned look will be even more damaging!

Eat Something

Picture this scene. David Hartman has just introduced a prominent attorney on "Good Morning America." David asks her a question and, although she was extremely glib and at ease in the Green Room, she stammers for an answer. David asks her another question, and instead of answering, she leans back in the chair and her eyes roll up. "Are you OK?" David asks. Unable to answer, the attorney just shakes her head.

David leans forward, takes her hands, and begins gently slapping her wrists to get her pulse going.

"We'll be going to commercial now," he says, and we do just that. As this dramatic scene is unfolding live on camera, a unit manager is phoning 9-1-1 for an ambulance, and one arrives before the commercial break has ended. The attorney, who now says she merely felt light-headed for a moment and blames the bright, hot television lights, agrees to go to nearby Roosevelt Hospital's emergency room.

Later in the day, she returns to the office to let us all know she is OK. She says, "My mother always said breakfast was the most important meal of the day. She never told me how important." She had had no breakfast, and her blood sugar level dropped sharply, leaving her light-headed and feeling faint. No doubt the stress of the interview environment, which can be an intimidating situation even to those who are experienced interviewees, exacerbated her problem.

Pay attention to what you eat before an interview. Physicians to whom I've spoken recommend complex carbohydrates (like fruit) and avoidance of processed sugars, which can make you lethargic. You also should avoid alcoholic beverages before an interview; their reputed calming qualities are not worth the risk. I've seen more than a few interview subjects show up drunk and slur their way through a conversation with a reporter. It's probably a good idea to avoid carbonated beverages, too. You don't want to be sitting on camera or in front of a radio microphone stifling belches.

Arrive Early

On the morning of Ronald Reagan's first inauguration, January 21, 1981, we were broadcasting "Good Morning America" from a studio built atop a high scaffold overlooking the White House. Our first guest for the day—in our 7:00 to 7:30 half hour—was Senator Barry Goldwater. At about 5:30 in the morning, as technicians were still doing last-minute checks of gear and David Hartman and the producers were beginning to do a final read-through of the script, one of our staffers burst into the studio and said, "Senator Goldwater's here. He's climbing the stairs." The stairs in this case went three stories straight up without any landings for catching your breath. Knowing that Senator Goldwater had recently had hip surgery, I ran out to intercept him before he climbed all those steps. I wanted to tell him that he was extremely early and might be more comfortable waiting at street level. I was too late; I caught him about halfway up the stairs.

"Oh, it's OK," he said. "I always arrive early." "We don't have a Green Room up there," I said. "That's OK. I'll sit in the corner and read the papers," he said. Under his arm he was carrying several newspapers. Once inside the studio, he took a seat in the back of the small room and read the newspapers he had brought, then the senator read the newspapers we had on hand, and finally—when we were finished with all our briefings—he talked informally with David Hartman and Steve Bell, the show's news anchor.

Goldwater, a media pro, arrived early for several good reasons. He was ensuring he'd be on time, he'd be oriented to the surroundings in which the interview would take place, he'd be informed (the newspapers), and he'd have ample opportunity to review any prepared messages he might have brought with him. Also, he could chat up his interviewers in advance.

Arriving early is especially important for broadcast interviews. There is nothing worse than rushing into a radio or television studio at the last minute, sitting down, and trying to respond to that first question while you are still catching your breath. Chances are good you'll be so harried that you won't convey your messages effectively.

Warm Up

As Senator Goldwater did, chat with the reporter before your interview. Consider it a mental stretching exercise or warm-up before you run your race. If it's a television interview, introduce yourself to the crew, too. Some TV reporters, following a rigid caste system, will not introduce you to these people, but don't let their rudeness stop you. The camera crew and lighting technicians can make you look good or bad, and if you've taken the trouble to say hello to them, they'll treat you better than if you snub them. A skilled practitioner of this tactic was Rosalynn Carter, former president Jimmy Carter's wife. Once during the 1976 presidential campaign, Mrs. Carter was a guest on "Good Morning America." She took the time during the commercial before her appearance to walk up to each cameraman, stagehand, and technician and introduce herself. When she sat down for that interview, if she had had a single strand of hair out of place, there were ten people on the set who would have put things right. After the interview Mrs. Carter made the rounds again and thanked each person on the set.

Be Discreet

It is very important, when you're chatting up the cast and crew, you don't say anything you wouldn't want the entire world to know. ("Boy, is this company having an awful quarter. I don't know if we can avoid bankruptcy. But you won't ask me about that, will you?") Of course you wouldn't do that, right? Well, don't be too sure. I once heard an actress say, "You know, I won't talk about my relationship with X, so don't even bother asking." An early question in the interview was, "You've said you won't talk about your relationship with X. Well, why won't you talk about it?" She wasn't asked about the relationship; the reporter respected her wishes in a literal sense. But the question that was asked sounded a lot more damaging. So instead of talking about what you can't say, use the warm-up for what you can—and want to—say.

A good hard-and-fast rule is this: whenever you are in proximity to a journalist, you are being interviewed. A print reporter can hear a quote, remember it, and write it down after the fact and use it in her article. A broadcast reporter can quote something you've said to her away from the microphone: "Off camera, Ms. Marmot confided to me that Ynot Company is on the brink of bankruptcy."

So if there exists the danger of being overly confidential, why bother with the warm-up before the interview? Because this is a great opportunity to plant some of your IMSs and to suggest questions that will elicit those IMSs. Just as you have an agenda for the interview, having an agenda for the warm-up can also work for you.

Shortly before President Nixon's resignation in 1974, I produced a story called "The Business of Watergate" for ABC News's weekly magazine show "The Reasoner Report." The story told how various Watergate figures were cashing in on their notoriety by writing books and giving lectures about the break-in and subsequent cover-up. I was to interview James McCord, one of the Watergate burglars, about his book *A Piece of Tape*. While the crew set up the lights and camera in his office in the Washington suburbs, McCord began talking to me about the break-in and gave a couple details that I'd not heard or read before. So when the camera was rolling, I asked him about them. He repeated them—in the context of their being revealed for the first time in his book. We both went away happy. I had some never-before-revealed pieces of the Watergate puzzle on film, and McCord had a plug for his book. He had used his warm-up time with me most effectively.

Don't Assume You Have Friends in the Media

Does this mean that even though you've been friendly with reporters in the past, you can't ever be relaxed and open with them? Unfortunately, yes. To illustrate this point, take the case of Spiro Agnew.

Agnew was gregarious and outgoing, with a ready smile and a relaxed manner. He'd been the governor of Maryland, and in 1968 Richard M. Nixon selected him to be his vice presidential running mate. Agnew, a pit bull on the stump, charmed the boys on the bus, the reporters covering the campaign. In later years he would become the bane of the press corps' existence, the Nixon administration's point man in its war on the media. Reporters, Agnew would charge in a famously pugnacious 1980 San Diego speech, were "nattering nabobs of negativism." (His exact words were "In the United States today, we have more than our share of the nattering nabobs of negativism.")

But in the early days, Agnew's relations with the reporters covering him were far less confrontational and antagonistic. Agnew was one of the guys. They may not have agreed with his politics, but the boys liked him and perhaps he even thought of them as friends. He certainly thought of Gene Oishi, a Japanese-American reporter who worked for the *Baltimore Sun*, as a friend, given that he had known Oishi since his days as governor of Maryland.

One day, Agnew asked the other reporters where "the fat Jap" was. Oishi—possibly because he was aware the remark was a joke, possibly because he was not present when the remark was made—was unwilling to break the story. Others were willing, and several days after Agnew's quip, the *Washington Post* ran the story, forcing Agnew into making an embarrassing apology.

Agnew had thought he'd been joking among friends. However, despite Oishi's reluctance to report the candidate's remark, the other reporters did what they saw as their professional duty.

Following commandments 1 and 2 will prepare you to make your points in any interview. By creating your own agenda, you'll gain confidence and avoid the disappointment of missed media opportunities. Knowing what you will and won't say is fundamental to media success. Your overall effectiveness as a spokesperson depends on having an agenda of messages that you want the reporter's audience to absorb, making those messages as relevant as possible, and expressing those messages with an effective presentation. Now let's move on to the commandments that concern how you're going to deliver those messages: the performance commandments.

CHAPTER 3

THE PERFORMANCE COMMANDMENTS

In our last chapter we dealt with preparedness commandments—the rules you must obey when formulating your intentional message statements. The next three commandments deal with delivering those messages to the media's audiences. I call these the performance commandments because—as noted earlier—an interview should be thought of as a performance, and heeding these edicts will make you a better performer. These three commandments are:

Thou shalt be quoteworthy.
Thou shalt practice, practice, practice.
Thou shalt not lie, evade, nor cop an attitude.

Marshall McLuhan, who was celebrated as the "oracle of the electronic age," coined the phrase "The medium is the massage." He turned it into the title of a book, and that title—almost universally misread as *The Medium Is the Message* (with an *e* rather than an *a*)—has licensed an entire generation of spokespersons to think that merely getting their face on television or their name in print is successfully delivering their message. In the first place, the term and the title are a play on words; McLuhan used the word *massage*, not the word *message*. The wordplay involves two meanings: "the medium is the mass age," or, more literally, the medium massages our brains just as a masseuse kneads our muscles. With all due respect to the late professor McLuhan, I suggest that for our purposes, we continue the misconstruction of his little pun, call it "message," and turn it on its side. When you are a spokesperson, your message is the message, and the medium is just that: your mechanism for delivering the message. But, with a nod of recognition to McLuhan's pun, the medium does require us to *ma*ssage our m*e*ssage in order to express it most effectively. Each of the different media demands we slightly temper, alter, and tailor our message to accommodate its unique attributes. More on those unique aspects of the different media in succeeding chapters. But for now, let's concentrate on the universal rules for all of the media—rules that begin with the three performance commandments.

Commandment 3: Thou Shalt Be Quoteworthy

In the previous chapter I wrote about being disappointed when I read the result of my phone conversation with the newspaper columnist who interviewed me about a situation at ABC News. He had used no direct quotes but merely paraphrased my remarks, and I felt I had been a dull and ineffective spokesperson. I had not taken advantage of the opportunity to get any message to his readers because I had prepared no message for those readers. I had no agenda—no intentional message statements to expound. And whatever expounding I did do in the service of his agenda had not been quoteworthy material. In broadcasting terms, I had not spoken in soundbites. After that second interview I began paying extremely close attention to what was directly quoted in newspapers and magazine stories. I listened closely to television news reports for the same thing. I wanted to know what determined when the interview subject's soundbite was used and when the correspondent felt compelled to paraphrase her.

What began as a casual investigation into my own shortcomings during a ten- or fifteen-minute phone interview became a thirty-year study. To this day I never read a newspaper, listen to a radio newscast, or watch a TV news program without mentally grading the interview subjects.

Some get an F; they fail miserably. You can tell this group very quickly: usually, not a word of what they said is in direct quotes in a print story. If they are part of a television report, they may be seen talking on camera, but their words are muted and the correspondent is telling us what they said. This is because they have expressed themselves so badly that their actual words are unusable.

A few nights ago, on the local news, I watched just such a "silent interview" in the sports report. A basketball coach was seen on camera, his lips were moving, and, I'm sure when it was taped, sounds were emerging from his mouth. None of those sounds made it to air. Instead, the reporter, speaking in voice-over above the muted lip-flapping coach, told us what he had said. Apparently the coach had spoken so ineptly that the reporter had to supply a comprehensible version for viewers. The fact that the reporter used no game or practice footage to cover the interview made the coach's failure much more dramatic. As a viewer, a producer, and a media trainer, I gave the hapless coach a failing grade.

The majority of interview subjects earn a mediocre C. There may be a direct quote from them in print, but most likely it's just a sentence or a sentence fragment. The C interview subjects may get eight or nine seconds of soundbites on television or radio, but often their statements aren't even complete sentences and the correspondent is compelled to chime in to clarify or amplify.

A handful earn an A. They are quoted profusely in print. In the electronic media, whole sentences—indeed, whole paragraphs—run uninterrupted. A classic A interview subject is former surgeon general C. Everett Koop. Imposing, deep-voiced, poised, and—most important—comprehensible, this physician's camera-side manner was probably an outgrowth of a comforting and competent bedside manner when he was a practicing clinician. News stories concerning Dr. Koop were inevitably filled with direct quotes. Television stories featured frequent soundbites. Dr. Koop, by being an A interview subject, in effect wrote the journalists' stories for them.

Aside from its appeal to our competitive instincts, why strive for an A in an interview? What's wrong with a comfortable C? For that matter, is it a crime to flunk? No, it's not a crime to flunk. You won't be left back or do detention or have to write an essay or take a makeup test. But a failing grade means you've not communicated as effectively as you should; you've missed an opportunity to directly sell your ideas, company, product, or organization to a wide audience. And, as we all should know, when we are paraphrased, there is abundant opportunity for misinterpretation.

The A interviewee, like Dr. Koop, is in control. He takes advantage of the opportunity an interview affords to reach a wide audience with ideas, programs, projects, or products described in his own words. To a large extent, the C, and more so the F, interviewee is missing out on that opportunity. He is not in control and is dependent on the reporter to help him convey an idea. And the reporter may not accommodate him. Through ineptitude, indifference, or even malice, the reporter may misconstrue, misinterpret, or misstate the message. Many of my media-training clients have told me that past interviewers "got it wrong," inaccurately conveying their messages. If you force the journalist to filter your ideas because you don't express them clearly, there is always the risk that her filter will distort what you want to say. An A interview subject keeps control by being quoteworthy, eliminating much of the reportorial filtering process.

To be quoteworthy you need to speak in soundbites. A soundbite is the mass media's most valuable commodity—a short, pithy, meaningful statement, a verbal headline.

Soundbites

Many decry soundbite journalism as bad journalism. They charge that it's vapid, glib, and oversimplified. The soundbite is the curse of television news and proof of the medium's superficiality. We know that because the print media tell us so, often quoting critics in—er—soundbite-length direct quotations. Take, for example, "Television news is soundbite journalism. And soundbite journalism is infantile, puerile, and futile." A pretty good quote, which, if lifted from the printed page and uttered on TV or radio, would be a soundbite! A good soundbite is a sentence, or two or three, that captures attention, delivers a message, and does so in a way that's sufficiently dramatic or witty to remain in your memory for a while. In a report on a tornado that devastated a small Southern town, the *New York Times* quoted a fourth-grader as saying, "The good news is we don't have school tomorrow. The bad news is we don't have a school." That's a good, effective soundbite from a nine- or ten-year-old. You'll remember that one a lot longer than a quote that reads, "Our school was blown down in the tornado and now we don't have a school to go to anymore." The fact that the first quote was in a newspaper and not on television or radio is telling. In point of fact, soundbites have been around forever. We just didn't call them soundbites until the electronic media came on the scene. Shakespeare's plays are full of soundbites ("Neither a borrower, nor a lender be"). And so is the Bible ("The wages of sin is death"). Try on the following classic soundbites for size:

"Give me liberty or give me death."
—Patrick Henry (1775)

"I only regret that I have but one life to lose for my country."
—Nathan Hale, on the gallows before being hanged by the British as a colonial spy (1776)

"Here I stand; I can do no other."
—Martin Luther (1521)

"The only thing we have to fear is fear itself."
—President Franklin D. Roosevelt (1933)

"I shall return."
—General Douglas MacArthur, upon retreating from the Philippines in World War II (1942)

"It's a recession when your neighbor loses his job; it's a depression when you lose yours."
—Former president Harry S. Truman (1956)

All those soundbites predate television news, and three of them predate any electronic media—and the discovery of electricity, for that matter!

Soundbites are the stuff of history and of all journalism. In fact, newspapers and magazines call them direct quotes. Here's a little homework: the next time you're spending a relaxing Sunday reading the newspaper or your favorite magazine, compare the amount of text in a story that's within quotation marks with the amount of text that is not. When you read the directly quoted material, assess the amount and quality of information in those quotes. Usually, direct quotes will share two attributes: good solid, comprehensible information and a deft turn of phrase. You can find direct quotes in which one or the other of these attributes will be present. But in those cases, you'll notice it's more likely that the deft turn of phrase will be directly quoted rather than the inelegantly phrased information-filled sentence. The vast majority of the words in any given article you'll read in this Sunday assignment are not direct quotes; the only words directly quoted are the most significant, the most trenchant statements—in other words, the soundbites. The *New York Times* celebrates and anoints the best daily soundbite in its Quote of the Day. Over the course of a month I kept careful score of the Quote of the Day; during that period the average length of the soundbite was less than thirty words. Most were no more than two sentences.

Many newspapers isolate direct quotes from stories and put them in italic boldface, box them like this, and then plant the box in the middle of a field of gray to highlight them.

Perfecting a Soundbite

Looking back at the masters of soundbites—Shakespeare, the ancients who crafted the Bible, John F. Kennedy, Harry Truman, General MacArthur, Patrick Henry, and so many others—we can see that there is nothing intrinsically wrong with answering a question with a soundbite, especially if it serves your purpose by vividly expressing your message. Soundbite journalism gets a bad rap because it is considered "short-shrift" journalism—superficial reporting and writing. Also, many soundbites are really bad because they are vapid slogans conveying little substance. This is not necessarily because the interviewee doesn't know her area of expertise. The more likely explanation is that she wasn't properly trained to make the most of her media opportunity.

Intentional Message Statements

You've already mastered the first step in producing a good soundbite by building the basis for the soundbite—your intentional message statement. In the last chapter you created five IMSs and tailored them to answer the audience's "Why should I care" question. You should now revisit these messages because you will use them as the basis for your soundbites.

All you need to do is hone your IMSs so they have fine, sparkling razorlike edges and deliver them in an assertive, positive manner without temporizing, compromising, or stumbling. If this sounds daunting, it can be, but only if you don't take the time to prepare. As noted previously, an interview is a performance and the benefits of preparing for that performance are well worth the effort. Part of that preparation is working on your soundbites in advance of every interview.

Look back at those historical soundbites cited a little earlier in this chapter. They are uniformly direct, concise, and bold. If you think you've made your soundbite too strong, it's probably on the verge of becoming a good soundbite; make it stronger—and shorter. The longest soundbite I quoted was Truman's witty line about the difference between a recession and a depression. It's a mere sixteen words long— sixteen words that are as meaningful today as they were when he delivered them about half a century ago! And it is very sharply honed. Compare Truman's line with a less effective alternate that expresses exactly the same idea:

Truman: "It's a recession when your neighbor loses his job; it's a depression when you lose yours."

Alternate: "It's a recession when your neighbor is out of work; it's a depression when you are."

The difference is that President Truman's soundbite is in the active voice, whereas the alternative is in the passive: "loses his job" versus "is out of work." The active verb *loses* is so much more powerful than the passive statement of a condition.

FDR's "fear" soundbite, "The only thing we have to fear is fear itself," is only ten words long. (It is frequently misquoted in eight words: "We have nothing to fear but fear itself.") Roosevelt was reading his first inaugural address, and it is likely this memorable quote was the result of fine-tuning by accomplished speechwriters—Roosevelt had successful poets and playwrights on his speechwriting staff. Some of the other vintage soundbites I quoted came from prepared remarks, too. But you need not hire speechwriters or poets to do this work, and you do not have to read your soundbites. After all, the other soundbites I quoted were spoken spontaneously.

Harry Truman, in particular, had a gift for concise and trenchant off-the-cuff remarks, making him a master of the soundbite. He famously said, "If you can't stand the heat, get out of the kitchen." Another of his favorites was "The buck stops here." He even had a small plaque on his presidential desk that read "The buck stops here." Compare that with similar sentiments expressed far less effectively by George W. Bush: "Presidents, whether things are good or bad, always get the blame." One is an historic soundbite, and the other wound up in a book called *Bushisms*, a compendium of presidential verbal gaffes. Both quotes have essentially the same meaning; it is the memorable language that differentiates them.

In my media-training sessions, I've always urged participants not to memorize their answers. I make an exception for brief soundbites. Unless you've got Harry Truman's unique gift, you'd better plan, write, and rehearse these particular ad-libs.

But please, don't do as our current crop of politicians do and, upon finding a resonating soundbite, repeat it ad nauseam for the same audience. Remember Al Gore's Social Security lockbox? He used the term so often that it lost its meaning and became a joke. Patrick Henry didn't go around the colonies repeating, "Give me liberty or give me death." He said it once in 1775, and it reverberates to this day.

In general, you can repeat a good soundbite until it runs nationally or until it becomes a cliché. At that point, let the media use the term for you. "Lockbox" would have been OK on a Houston radio station, then in a Denver newspaper, and later on in a TV newscast in Chicago. But as soon as it was on the network nightly newscasts and on CNN once or twice, Gore probably should have dropped it.

Do you remember Senator Bob Dole's oft-repeated soundbite with his prescription for eliminating the narcotics problem, which he unleashed during his 1996 presidential campaign? Following leaks to the media that candidate Dole was going to unveil a "powerful new slogan to help fight the war on drugs," the senator came out with, "Just don't do it." On the stump he didn't just say it once—he would say it four, five, even six times in rapid succession, turning it into a kind of manic chant. The words might have worked in a one-on-one interview—a masterpiece of brevity in answer to a question. But as a chant, it was not merely seriously wanting; it became comedic.

Speak in Complete Sentences

How is it our candidates make so many media mistakes that their utterances become the currency of comedy? Media critic Michael Wolff, writing in the December 9, 2002, issue of *New York Magazine*, summed up the situation this way: "All but an exceptional few politicians suck at making, or understanding, media. This is a surprise, because the only thing politicians want to do is get on TV. That's their basic job. But they're talentless. They're zeros. The media consultants they hire to help them are mostly hacks and rejects, too." In fact, Wolff may be too hard on my colleagues. The paradigm of a long-gone past—making the exact same speech at every venue—remains a constant in political campaigns to this day. It is a paradigm that was established before there were national media that electronically spread every quote and speech nationwide. The same is true for campaign interviews. Too often politicians give the same word-for-word answers to questions. There's nothing wrong with reusing a good answer for new audiences. But when those answers are broadcast repeatedly to the same audience, our politicians look overly scripted.

Today, one thing most politicians have mastered is the art of speaking in complete sentences; during an interview you should, too. From a practical media-management point of view, speaking in complete sentences enhances your control of the interview because the print reporter won't have to add the missing words in brackets and the broadcast reporter won't have to write a tortured lead-in to your soundbite. Speaking in complete sentences gives you the opportunity of having longer and uninterrupted broadcast soundbites or printed quotes, which will help you capture the viewer's or reader's full attention.

Also, it's usually a good idea to incorporate the sense of the question in your answer. Doing this gives you greater control over the way your answer is used; in fact, it virtually preempts the reporter from using her question either in broadcast or in print. In other words, if asked, "How's the weather today," don't answer, "It's fine." Answer, instead, "The weather today is fine." An added benefit is that when you include the sense of the question in your answer, you buy yourself a little bit of thinking time to decide which of your intentional message statements you want to unleash in response. Former presidents Nixon, Reagan, and Clinton were particularly gifted at incorporating the sense of the question in their answers. If you listen to the soundbites from their news conferences, you'll notice that their statements almost always stood on their own; you understood what they were responding to without having to hear the question. I wrote that it is "usually" a good idea to incorporate the sense of the question in your answer. The exception to that rule is the loaded, hostile, negative question like, "Wasn't your failure to alert your investors to the downturn in sales a case of managerial malfeasance?" Incorporating the sense of that question into your answer—even if the answer is a ringing denial—would be counterproductive.

Earlier, I urged you to be concise and bold with your soundbites. You can be too bold. Years ago as a print reporter, I covered a news conference by the leader of the Brooklyn dockworkers local 1814, the combative "Tough Tony" Anastasio. A confrontation was brewing with the shippers association, and, on this particular day, Tough Tony, who looked like everyone's grandfather but who spoke like a character out of "The Sopranos," told the assembled reporters, cameras, and microphones that if there were not a new contract soon, "The docks is gonna run red wit blood." His glib and polished second in command, Tony Scotto, who was also Tough Tony's son-in-law, interjected, "What Pop means is . . ."

To those of us covering the news conference, what "Pop" meant was abundantly clear. But I submit that while it was a great soundbite for those of us in the media, it may not have been for Anastasio. It made him appear to be a ruthless thug. If you need a "handler" to spin your soundbite, you probably should not have uttered it in the first place.

Additionally, I would caution all spokespersons against "red wit blood"–style soundbites. You really want to avoid being quoted as threatening or condoning any sort of illegal activity. If the activity were to come to pass, even without your involvement, your soundbite could be extremely embarrassing—even incriminating. And while it is true that the public's memory is distressingly short, the media's memory is limitless. They keep everything. Anything you ever say to the media can be found in an archive and then reprinted or rebroadcast.

Additional Tips for Being Quoteworthy

Here are some additional tips that will help you obey the quoteworthy commandment. They will make your broadcast soundbites and printed quotes more effective and memorable:

Lead with your strongest stuff.
Keep it short and simple.
Activate your jargon filter.
Establish your brand.
"Yes" is not an answer. Neither is "No."
Use grabbers.

Lead with Your Strongest Stuff

Copy the media's technique and speak the way the media write. Read a news story or listen to a newscast and pay special attention to how the stories are structured. Typically, there is a headline, then a lead sentence, and then supporting facts. The lead sentence is the one that contains the most important information the reporter wishes to convey. For most of us, it is counterintuitive to express ourselves this way in conversation. Normally when we're asked a question, the progression of our answer is this: fact A plus fact B, therefore conclusion C. When we are communicating through the media, we must reverse that: conclusion C because fact A plus fact B. While it may seem illogical to answer questions this way, there are valid reasons for doing it. In electronic media, the listener or viewer doesn't have the advantage that a newspaper or magazine reader has—the ability to go back and reread a quote. I call this the reread factor. For electronic media, it's crucial to get the most important elements up front to set the audience's mental agenda. But use it for print interviews, too, because you'll be speaking to the reporter exactly the way he writes his stories—and speaking this way makes it much more likely you'll wind up in direct quotes rather than being paraphrased. Also, as a former print reporter, I can attest that my notes were always extremely legible at the start of a response and became more and more difficult to read as the answer progressed. You want to get the top ideas out before writer's cramp sets in. (It's worth noting that FDR's "The only thing we have to fear is fear itself" was the fifth sentence in a twenty-minute speech.)

KISS (Keep It Short and Simple)

Why short? Because if you go on and on and on and on and on and on and on . . . Get the point? If you go on and on in a broadcast interview, you're going to lose your listener's interest and she'll forget how you started. In a print interview, that listener who's going to lose interest is the reporter. Why simple? Because if it's too complicated, your WSIC (Why Should I Care) quotient dwindles. How short and how simple? As to length, I urge my clients to keep their responses to less than a minute! A thirty-second answer is even better. You'd be surprised how much you can say in thirty seconds. As a test, begin reading this paragraph out loud starting with the word *KISS*. Have someone time you, stopping you when you get to thirty seconds. Reading out loud at an unhurried, but not funereal, pace, I reached the words *quotient dwindles* in just under thirty seconds. I was able to convey my entire message about the need for brevity in that time.

As to how simple you should make your answers, let me relate a story my friend Kerry Millerick told me. Kerry, a producer and very funny on-camera talent, was working on a television show with a highly respected veteran producer when he used the word *acknowledge* in a script. "You can't use that word," thundered the highly respected one. "Why? Everyone knows what it means," protested Kerry. "I mean, we're trying to communicate on the level of a twelve-year-old, aren't we? Every twelve-year-old knows what acknowledge means." "Twelve?" bellowed the highly respected producer. "Who told you twelve? It's five. Five, not twelve." With all due respect to the highly respected producer, I think he was aiming way too low. How simple you keep it really depends on what your audience can absorb. So whether you tailor your remarks for the twelve-year-old, the twenty-one-year-old, the mass market, or the sophisticated consumer, your level of simplicity or complexity depends on your ultimate audience, the reader or listener of the particular interview you're about to do. As commandment 2 dictated, you need to know to whom you are speaking. Thus a financial analyst's response to a question on CNN's "Lou Dobbs Tonight" (formerly called "Moneyline") should be more sophisticated than an answer to a similar question on "The Today Show" because Dobbs's audience is likely to be much more knowledgeable about the whys and wherefores of finance than the average "Today Show" viewer. One of my greatest challenges, both as a reporter and as a media trainer, has been to get scientists to speak simply enough for the science-deprived to understand what they're talking about. It is one thing for a scientist to speak to her peers in a science or technical journal. They'll get her message. It's quite another for her to explain her work in *USA Today*. And in a general-audience broadcast, it is even more difficult. I've found most of them can rise to the challenge if they focus intently on just who their audience is.

Activate Your Jargon Filter

Every business, science, art, and trade has its own jargon. You and your colleagues may understand what all those acronyms stand for and may instantly comprehend the catchy lingo, but the people you're trying to reach generally do not. A good reporter will stop you and ask you to define terms. But that interrupts the flow of thought and steals time better spent casting forth your messages. That said, some acronyms have become universally understood and don't need explaining. People may wonder what entity you're talking about if you said, "The National Aeronautics and Space Administration," but they will instantly know "NASA." Similarly, FBI and CIA are universally familiar. But most acronyms mystify and most jargon is indecipherable. Again, it depends upon your ultimate audience, but if you must err, then err on the side of jargon-free answers rather than jargon-cluttered answers. And if you must use an acronym, define it after first usage: "At FEMA—or the Federal Emergency Management Agency—we have teams that can be on the scene of any natural disaster within hours after it occurs, even if roads are closed and public transportation has been crippled."

Establish Your Brand

How many times have you tuned in midinterview and heard an author on radio or television refer repeatedly to "my book" or "the book." Even if he captured your interest, you're going to have a tough time at Barnes and Noble or Waldenbooks getting even the most helpful clerk to find *The Book* or *My Book*. Music artists frequently talk about "my CD" or "my album." When they do that, I tell them I'm going to bring out a CD of my own called *My CD* and another called *My Album* because they've been helping me promote it. Similarly, how many times have you heard an interview subject say "we" instead of giving the name of his company or organization? "We" is not a name. Try, instead, "We at Consolidated Ynot feel . . ." If it's got a name, use it.

Think about the photographs of competitive skiers you see in the sports pages of your daily newspaper. When you see one holding her skis right next to her head, you'll see the logo side facing the camera. The skier in the photo is branding—planting the name of her ski company sponsor in your head and implying that if you wear her brand, you'll ski as well as she does. There can be too much branding. Look at NASCAR race cars. If there were any more company logos on those cars, they wouldn't need to be painted. There are, in fact, so many logos that many of us don't pay attention to any of them. NASCAR drivers, too, are logo'd to the max. There is enough reading material on their uniform jackets to totally distract you from what they're saying.

The mandate to brand is somewhat less important when you're dealing with the print media—where there's that reread factor—but getting into good habits in one medium pays dividends in all media.

"Yes" and "No" Are Not Answers

"Yes" and "No" statements are the beginning of answers, the door openers to your real answer. You are not in a court of law. In an interview, there is no such thing as a "yes-or-no" question, even if one is asked that way. How many times have you seen an interview with an uncoached, unsophisticated individual who responds only with "yes" and "no" answers? In those instances the reporter is forced to fill in the blanks left by the interviewee—always a less-than-satisfactory solution. I can recall one such interview on "Good Morning America" when Joan Lunden was interviewing a woman who would just answer "Yes" to whatever Joan asked. So before her next question, Joan would fill in the blank.

> **Joan:** And so then you went to the hospital and you told them that your baby had a very high fever.
> **Guest:** Yes.
> **Joan:** And they admitted her?
> **Guest:** Yes.
> **Joan:** Then they told you it was pneumonia?
> **Guest:** Yes.
> **Joan:** But you didn't believe that?
> **Guest:** No.
> **Joan:** You thought your daughter might have an allergy to something she'd eaten?
> **Guest:** Yes.

Use Grabbers

A grabber is a phrase that makes your message come alive. A grabber can be a metaphor or simile. It can be a comparison, or it can be a quote or a paraphrase of a quote. A grabber can be an attention-getting fact, like a remarkable statistic. A grabber is any verbal turn of phrase that fixes your message in a listener's head by capturing her imagination. It can even be a very brief, illustrative anecdote. Here are some sample grabbers:

Comparison: "That NASCAR Ford bears about as much relationship to a showroom Crown Victoria as an eagle bears to a ladybug. They both fly, but they're different species."

Quote or paraphrase of a quote: "When preparing for an interview, borrow a thought from John F. Kennedy and ask not what you can do for the reporter's agenda; ask what the reporter can do for your agenda."

Metaphor: "This proposal is the *Titanic* of economic planning—big, ambitious, and doomed to sink."

Amazing fact or statistic: "When it came to architecture, the Romans got it right. Every stadium and arena in the world uses the very same entrance and exit designs of the Colosseum. And the Colosseum was built in about 80 A.D.—nearly two thousand years ago!"

Anecdote: "I asked my clients to tell me the downside of their new product before the news conference and they said, 'There isn't any.' I said, 'What would Ralph Nader ask if he came to the news conference?' and they replied, 'He'd ask if he could buy the product.' Well, they didn't prepare for the downside questions and they got clobbered."

Simile: "When the spokesman got flustered at the news conference, the response of the reporters was like the feeding frenzy of sharks."

Use worksheet 3 in the Appendix for developing grabbers for your IMSs, or you can create your own worksheets. Try to come up with one grabber for every one of your message statements. You'll want to take your time with this exercise; for most of us, grabbers don't just spring to mind. The simplest grabbers are comparisons and similes, so try for those first. The best way to craft a grabber is to ask yourself, "What everyday activity or concern can I equate with my message?" Thus you might come up with, "Having a corporation change its direction from being a growth stock company to a value stock company is about as hard as making a U-turn in a subway train."

After you've crafted your grabbers, read them out loud to make sure that they sound natural and that you're comfortable saying them. If you find them awkward, you'll want to massage them until they don't sound quite so foreign to you. Keep this worksheet handy and refine your grabbers over time. And always remember to jot down new grabbers as they occur to you. It's distressing to think about how many wonderful grabbers have been lost forever because their authors felt they could remember them the next time they did an interview and never bothered to commit them to paper or to a hard drive. It takes a great deal of preparation to be spontaneous in an interview, but the result is worth the investment in time and effort. Once you're ready with your IMSs and their supporting grabbers, you need to heed the next commandment.

Commandment 4: Thou Shalt Practice, Practice, Practice

I call this one the Carnegie Hall commandment, after an old joke by the late Henny Youngman: "Fella comes up to me on the street and says, 'Hey, how do I get to Carnegie Hall?' I says, 'Practice, practice, practice.'"

If you are wondering how you practice for an interview when you don't know what you'll be asked, the answer is that, with a little effort, you can usually figure out the questions an interviewer will pose to you. If you did the homework in the last chapter—watched the TV show, read the newspaper or magazine, listened to the radio show—you should have a pretty solid idea of the attitude, level of sophistication, and point of view of your interviewer.

So now it's time to write out his questions so you can practice, practice, practice your answers. But do yourself a favor and don't write questions like, "Gosh, you are a great fellow coming from a great organization. What can you tell me about yourself and your organization that makes you and it so admirable?"

While a handful of interviewers might ask something akin to such a puffball question (CNN's Larry King is one; he's kind and polite to virtually all his guests save ax murderers and toxic waste dumpers), you'd better count on getting challenging questions. Even the most benign reporter can ask a tough question. Here is Merlis's Law of Interviews (a scientific certainty as immutable as the First Law of Thermodynamics or Murphy's Law): anyone unprepared for tough questions will be asked tough questions.

Remember my anecdotal grabber in the last section, about the clients who didn't prepare for downside or hostile questions? It's a true story about a financial product rolled out at first only in California, where the disastrous news conference took place. Interestingly, a year after the statewide introduction of the product there was a national rollout at a New York news conference, and this time the clients drilled extensively, developing persuasive answers to tough questions. They were ready for combat; this time no onslaught was going to take them by surprise. Curiously enough, nothing happened at the New York news conference. Perhaps lulled by the huge buffet breakfast the client laid out, the New York and national reporters didn't ask a single tough question. But it's better to be prepared for the tough ones and *not* get them than to be unprepared and be assaulted with them.

In the next chapter we'll work up a list of tough questions and I'll teach you how to get from a challenging question to your IMSs. You'll need that information before you begin to practice, practice, practice. For now though, let me give you some techniques for practicing.

If you've ever prepared for a speech by sitting at your desk silently reading your text, you know that's not practice. It is amazing how sentences over which the eye and the brain can gracefully glide become unspeakable—literally—when read aloud. The brain can handle tongue-trippers, but the mouth can't.

By the same token, the best way to practice for an interview is by speaking out loud with a real, live questioner. Don't ask yourself the questions; you'll be too easy on yourself. Hearing the words coming from another voice, rather than from an internal one, will make them very real to you. Actors always run lines with another person—even if it isn't the individual with whom they'll do the scene. Running lines helps put those incoming words in a human context. In exactly the same way, hearing questions asked by someone else—even an excessively friendly someone else—is far more effective than imagining the questions coming from a phantom reporter.

Get a friend, family member, or colleague to pop questions at you. Videotape your responses and watch your performance—over and over. There is no substitute for seeing yourself in action, even if you're prepping for a magazine or newspaper interview.

Grade yourself. Keep your remote control nearby so you can frequently pause. Review the tape. Have your IMS and grabber worksheets in hand so you can see how many of them you worked into the interview. Equally important is to identify opportunities where you could have or should have inserted IMSs. Only by seeing your missed opportunities will you know how to take advantage of them in the future. Keep practicing until you can work in all your IMSs and grabbers. That's how to practice. But before you begin those dry runs, you'll need to learn the fifth commandment and you'll need to read Chapter 4, "Successful Interview Tools," to familiarize yourself with how interviews are used and how reporters use the tricks of their trade. You'll also learn the tricks of the interviewee's trade.

Commandment 5: Thou Shalt Not Lie, Evade, nor Cop an Attitude

Aside from the moral and ethical imperatives against lying or evading, there are very practical reasons not to do it—as evidenced by these two examples, which just happen to be soundbites:

"I did not have sexual relations with that woman."

—Bill Clinton

A nine-word soundbite with ramifications that rendered a presidency ineffective for months on end.

"Read my lips: no new taxes."

—George H. W. Bush

A six-word soundbite that went a long way toward costing the first President Bush a second term.

By way of explanation, let's refer to a soundbite that predates sound recording:

"It is true that you may fool all the people some of the time; you can even fool some of the people all the time; but you can't fool all of the people all the time."

—Abraham Lincoln

Not all lies and other shadings of fact will be found out, but recent history shows just how damaging they can be when the light of truth shines on them. In a strict dictionary sense, President Clinton was not lying but rather was just evading—fooling the people—since Webster's definition of "sexual relations" is the act of coitus. You'll note the president did not say, "I did not have sex with that woman," but instead said, "I did not have sexual relations with that woman." He wasn't lying, but he was shading the truth.

In the same vein, how costly was it for Martha Stewart, when she was first accused of insider trading, to have put forth a story about previously instructing her broker to sell her ImClone stock when it dropped below $60 a share? How much more forgiving would the public have been had she said, "In the excitement of the moment, knowing what I knew, I made a mistake by acting on advance information. It was an unfortunate mistake, and to make amends, I am donating the entire profit I made from that sale to the American Cancer Society."? When

Ms. Stewart finally did do an interview, she spoke with the *New Yorker* magazine—two months after the charges first surfaced—and she declined to discuss the details of the case on the record. The interview was conducted by *New Yorker* legal correspondent Jeffrey Toobin, who as the son of a former colleague of mine, Marlene Sanders of ABC and later CBS News, appears to have journalism in his genes. In the interview, Ms. Stewart appeared most concerned about the public's perception of her but did nothing to court public opinion, repeatedly lacing her quotes with egotistical comments. In other words, she copped an attitude—a pitfall we'll deal with in a moment. In fact, the Martha Stewart *New Yorker* interview is a virtual textbook example of how *not* to do a print interview; Chapter 8 treats the subject in more detail.

There is another practical reason for telling the truth in interviews, and for that I quote one of my mentors, Elmer W. Lower, former president of ABC News. He used to say, "Always tell the truth. That way you won't have to remember what you said." (Incidentally, that's a good soundbite/grabber.)

In my earliest days at ABC News, before becoming a producer, I was the director of publicity for the division. A big story was about to break, and Elmer told me only that there was a big story coming, adding, "I'm not going to tell you anything about it so if you get a call from the press, you won't have to lie." The story was that ABC News had hired Harry Reasoner away from CBS News. Not fifteen minutes after Elmer told me he wasn't going to tell me what the big story was, I got a call from a Chicago newspaper columnist who asked me, "What's this story about Harry Reasoner leaving CBS News to become the anchor at ABC News?" I could honestly respond, "This is the first I've heard of it."

What if telling the truth in an interview can land you in jail or subject you to a lawsuit? That would appear on the surface to be a good question, but if either of these scenarios is at all likely, why is your lawyer letting you talk to the media at all? The news media, after all, unlike Congress and the state legislatures, cannot compel you to appear and talk to them. Silence is a more satisfying response than falsehood.

The third part of the fifth commandment—about not copping an attitude—ought to be self-evident. If you are not an angry young rebel actor, a gangsta rapper, or a professional wrestler (all role players), you do yourself a disservice by copping a hostile, challenging, superior, or arrogant attitude.

Vice President Al Gore's supercilious attitude in the first presidential debate in 2000 cost him dearly in the election. Had he shown some humility, he might have won enough additional electoral votes to have landed in the White House. Similarly, Martha Stewart's superior noblesse oblige attitude contributed to the media frenzy attendant upon her insider trading accusation. If you put a chip on your shoulder, the media will be more than happy to knock it off.

Now that we've gone over the five commandments of interviews and some interpretive analysis, let's move on to practical applications in interview settings. Let's first examine what you can expect to encounter and how you can turn the challenge of an interview into an opportunity to get your message out to a large and interested audience.

CHAPTER 4

SUCCESSFUL
INTERVIEW TOOLS

In Chapters 2 and 3 you learned how to prepare an agenda for an interview and how to tailor your messages for the media. Now let's look at the most basic media encounter, the interview. You'll want to master a specific set of tools—and understand the tricks of the reporter's trade—before submitting to any interview. Of course, not all interviews are similar in tone and attitude. Before sitting down face-to-face with the reporter or before taking her interview phone call, you will already have examined the outlet and, if possible, the work of the reporter for some clues about how your material will be used and how you may be treated in the interview and the subsequent story. There are also a few clues to a reporter's agenda that you'll want to investigate. You'll be a leg up on ascertaining her agenda if she's working on a story that was initiated by you or by your organization.

When you initiate the story—by making an announcement of a new discovery, product, or service—reporters are responding to your agenda, so it is usually easier to keep the session targeted. When you are responding to someone else's announcement or to an interviewer's enterprise story—that is, one she initiated herself—the initial agenda is in the reporter's hands. In those cases, it requires more work on your part to bring the questioning around to your agenda.

Most interviews are neutral or even friendly—not hostile and adversarial. But be aware that a friendly tone can mask a tough question. Not every inquisitorial reporter comes on with the pit bull determination and toughness of a Mike Wallace on "60 Minutes." In fact, some of the most effective investigative reporters *don't* grip you by the neck and squeeze; rather, they cordially invite you to hang yourself.

One of the best investigative television correspondents I ever knew was David Schoumacher, who worked for both CBS News and ABC News. I worked with David at ABC and observed that he was a master at asking the toughest questions in the friendliest way. He had a warm and charming smile, and his tone never became challenging or prosecutorial. As a result, he was able to get an amazing array of skilled corporate executives and politicians to make incriminating statements in the most matter-of-fact way. Because they were not on the defensive, their protective radar was off and they regularly gave up more information than they ever intended.

Early in the twentieth century, Ida M. Tarbell, the mother of investigative journalism, worked for years to research her book *The History of the Standard Oil Company*. It was her masterwork, revealing the illegal practices used by John D. Rockefeller to monopolize the oil industry in the United States. At the time, most men felt a woman's capacity to grasp complex business concepts was extremely limited, so many an executive opened up to the "little lady," never expecting that her steel-trap mind was not just grasping but was analyzing and understanding every nuance of what they were saying. The executives would probably have been far more on guard had they been dealing with a male journalist.

Why rehash this bit of ancient history? To emphasize the fact that the way someone looks or acts is not a clue to that person's goal. And, truth be told, sometimes the most benign reporter asks tough questions, even in the absence of malice.

For any recorded or print interview, you want to figure out—as far in advance as possible—how your participation fits into the larger picture the reporter is trying to create. To that end, you or your public relations aides should ask the five questions given in the following section. It's important you get your answers before the reporter gets hers. You can pose them when she calls to arrange the interview or, as a last resort, during the preinterview warm-up. Reporters are used to being asked all these questions and, more often than not, are perfectly willing to answer them. This need not be a long, drawn-out discussion;

most of the questions can be answered with just a few words by the reporter. Sometimes she'll tell you she doesn't know an answer. That may be truthful, because the story is a work in progress. Or that answer may be an obfuscation. If you don't get straight answers to three or four of these questions, you were probably misled about the nature and direction of the interview and you need to be especially on guard. Later in this chapter we'll review techniques for parrying a tough interview, but first let's go over some tips for learning in advance the nature of your forthcoming media encounter.

Five Key Questions to Ask a Reporter Before the Interview

Before the interview, there are five important questions you should ask your interviewer. The order of questions is immaterial, except for the first one, which sets the agenda and tone. Reporters rarely embark on a story before they know the answer to this one, so if there is an "I don't know" or "I'm not sure" answer, you should be on guard.

What Is the Direction and Thrust of the Story?

You should ask this in a helpful way; you want to be cooperative and outgoing. And, chances are, given the answer to this question you can, indeed, be much more helpful to the journalist. Try asking in a tone like this: "What is your story going to be about? I'd like to know so I can gather and review the appropriate materials and make sure I've got all the facts and figures straight." Most reporters want you to be prepared; if you do the research in advance, they don't have to do it after the fact. Often if an interview does go beyond what the reporter indicated in advance, it will be because it naturally flows there. There are, however, a number of reporters and producers—usually working on the investigative publications and broadcasts—who will not give you a straightforward answer to this question. Ostensibly that's because they want the interview to appear more spontaneous. But actually they want to give you as few clues to their agenda as possible so they can catch

you unawares and trap you. That's why it's helpful to review a particular reporter's prior work and learn about her reputation before agree-
ing to the interview. We'll have more on dealing with this breed of
reporter in Chapter 6, "Digging Deep: Investigative Broadcasts."

Who Else Are You Interviewing?

If he's interviewing four people from your company or organization,
you should tailor your answers accordingly. ("Well, you're going to be
talking to Sharon, and she is our authority on this issue. My own area
of specialization is . . .") If he tells you he's also going to be interviewing competitors or opponents, you have the opportunity to second-
guess what they've told him or will tell him and craft answers that
respond to critics while incorporating your IMSs. Also, knowing whom
else he's interviewing gives you the opportunity to suggest still more
interviewees—especially individuals who agree with your point of view.
You might say to him, "That's a good list, but you might also want to
talk to Dr. Hackley; he's the foremost independent authority in the
country on . . ."

How Much of My Time Will You Need?

Knowing the answer to this question enables you to set limits on the
length of the interview. If he says, "An hour," you can always say, "I'm
afraid I can only spare twenty minutes." Then, if the interview is going
well, stay the full hour. Be aware that reporters frequently will under-
state the amount of time they need because they hope that once you're
sitting with them, you'll feel awkward about ending the interview. But
if you've told him in advance how much time he has, then the control
rests with you. "Well, Jim, I told you I could spare fifteen minutes, and
we've been here for that fifteen minutes, so I'm afraid we've got to wrap
it up now." Of course, if it's going swimmingly, you can say, "I know I
told you I could only spare fifteen minutes for this interview, but I think
I can squeeze in another five if you need it." President Jimmy Carter's
national security adviser, Zbigniew Brzezinski, used to ask television

interviewers, "How long will this interview run on the air?" If they responded, "Six minutes," he started the timer on his wristwatch and at the end of six minutes removed the microphone—unless it was going really well, in which case six minutes sometimes magically became eight, nine, or ten minutes. Brzezinski was trying to prevent producers from editing his interviews, but when things were moving along smoothly for him, he gambled that he could deliver additional messages that would survive the editing process.

How Long Will Your Article (or Broadcast Story) Run?

You can be a lot more expansive and detailed in your answers if the interview is for a *New York Times Sunday Magazine* piece that will run seven thousand words than if it is for a two-minute report on the local TV station's 11 P.M. newscast. You need this information to help you frame your answers appropriately. A truly skilled interview subject like director Steven Spielberg, for example, gives a short form, quip of an answer to an interviewer who grabs him for a few seconds as he's walking down the Academy Awards red carpet on his way into the Oscar ceremony. Asked virtually the same question on Bravo Network's leisurely and informative "Inside the Actor's Studio," he will give a longer, contemplative, thought-provoking response. On the red carpet, he knows that his comment will be one of dozens used in the Oscar story, so he keeps it short; whereas the Bravo show will focus only on his thoughts and feelings, so he can be more expansive.

Do You Need or Want Any Documentation, Photographs, or Videotape?

If you know in advance what support material would be helpful, then you won't find yourself sitting across from the interviewer saying, "I have a paper on that. I wish I'd brought it with me." Or, "You know, I've seen a really good photograph that illustrates that point. I don't know where it is, but take my word for it—or take my thousand words for it—it was terrific." Even if she says she needs nothing, you might want to bring to your interview props and videotape (for television), photographs (for all media), and documentation. Naturally, you'll only be bringing props, videotape, photographs, and documentation that buttress your IMSs. As an example, not long ago, some astronomers were discussing how infrared telescopes enable us to see aspects of the universe that optical telescopes cannot see. Their message really came home to me when I discovered on NASA's website virtually identical pictures of Saturn taken through optical and infrared devices. In the infrared photo, the familiar ringed planet has brilliant auroras at its poles, planetary wonders totally invisible in the optical photographs. I encouraged the astronomers to bring these photos—or others like them—to future interviews to illustrate their point. And you should consider bringing similar visuals if you have compelling images that effectively illustrate or prove your point.

How to Master Any Interview

Media mastery begins with interview mastery. A simple set of skills can arm you with the confidence that you can work your agenda into any interview.

Enabling Your Agenda/Disabling the Reporter's Agenda

Your goal in an interview is to enable your agenda. As noted earlier, if the reporter's agenda meshes with yours, then it's relatively easy. If the reporter's agenda diverges from yours, you must first disable his agenda in order to enable yours.

In general, reporters are interested in what's new, unique, and unusual. The old cliché is that dog bites man is not news, but man bites dog is news. These days, however, there is a premium on bad and frightening news, so that dog bites man may once again be considered news— if the bite is severe enough and if enough dogs are biting enough men to frighten people with a threatening "trend." Conflict and drama pique the news reporter's interest. And good news—miracle cures, money-saving schemes or tips, and safety information—is also considered grist for the journalist's mill. Sometimes, then, your agenda will neatly match the reporter's needs—for instance, when you are promoting a book on saving money by reducing energy consumption in the home or you are giving information about how to safeguard the health of audience members with a new medication or medical procedure. At other times, you may be on the defensive—say when critics charge that a product, policy, or program you advocate is in some way dangerous, costly, or ineffective.

In either case, as with most of life's endeavors, the best defense is an offense. If you have followed the Boy Scout commandments in Chapter 2, then you know the IMSs you want to express in your interview, you are familiar with the tone and nature of the publication or broadcast, and you know to whom you are speaking and that person's level of sophistication. You are also prepared to answer questions in a short and simple manner, lead with your conclusion, and brand your answers.

Getting your message across to the skeptical WSIC (Why Should I Care) listener is pretty easy when the reporter asks, "Tell me, my friend, have you any intentional message statements you'd like my readers [viewers, listeners] to know about?" But in the ten thousand interviews I've conducted or overseen, I've never heard that question posed and I've certainly never asked it myself. While reporters never ask that question, the closest they come to it is the common interview ending: "That about covers my questions. Is there anything you feel I've left out or that my readers [viewers, listeners] should know?" That question is the equivalent of the "any intentional message statements" question I cited and is always to be answered with one of your IMSs—even if you've already used every one you brought into the interview with you. If you had five points at the outset and managed to work in only three or four of them, go to one of your unused message statements. If you've already managed to work in all of them before the "anything else" question, revisit one of them. Which one? Try either your most important IMS or one you think you may not have articulated very well. Maybe you'll say it better the second time, or maybe the repetition will put your IMS in mental boldface for the reporter. It never hurts to repeat the general thrust of an IMS, especially if you can express it in slightly different language the second time.

When it is asked, the "anything else" question always comes at the end of an interview—but there's no guarantee it will come. Because of this, you should pepper the whole session with your IMSs, not wait until the very end, hoping for the "anything else" question. The "anything else" question is rarely asked in live broadcast interviews; normally these interviews run a fixed length of time, and journalists use every moment of that time asking their questions. Also, broadcast interviewers don't like letting listeners think they may have left something out.

Four Steps from a Reporter's Question to Your IMS

Obviously, a direct question that solicits one of your IMSs is the easiest way to get one into an interview. "So tell me about this new asthma medication your company has developed" is an explicit invitation to enunciate an IMS. Similarly, if the reporter praises you, your company, or your product, that is an open door through which an IMS can step. "I'm hearing very good things from asthma patients about this new medication you've brought to market." The response is not, "Gee, thanks"; it is, instead, "Yes and that's because . . ." and continue on to an IMS.

If you finish answering a question and the reporter is searching his list of questions for his next query, you can fill the vacuum by saying, "Another thing that asthma sufferers will want to know is . . ." and go to another IMS. But a word of caution: filling in a pause is only to be used in a friendly interview. A time-honored trick of a hostile interviewer is to pause after you've responded to a tough question, in the hope you'll feel the pressure of the silence and go beyond the answer you intended to give. More on that later in this chapter.

But if the reporter is not asking puffball questions, not throwing kudos your way, and not searching a sheet of paper for his next question, what do you do? Well, you cannot do what Henry Kissinger did when he was secretary of state and sometimes began his briefings of

State Department reporters by announcing, "Ladies and gentlemen, I hope you have your questions because I have my answers." The State Department press corps was a club of sorts, and you can get away with that kind of thing in a club. Because most of us aren't in a club with the reporters who'll be questioning us, we must build a bridge between the question and our IMS using the following steps. Keep in mind that these four steps work together; you need to follow all four of them.

Step 1: Give a Short Form Answer

To keep a question from being asked again, you need to pay it some factual lip service. You don't want to appear blandly evasive. So acknowledge the question first. By acknowledging, I don't mean, "Gee, you should have asked me about Y instead of X, and here's my answer to Y." There is no quicker way to turn an interview hostile than by telling a reporter what she should be asking. Incredibly, some people in public life actually do that. Lyndon Johnson was famous for it. "No, no," he would say, "the question ought to be . . ." and he'd ask himself a question he wanted to answer. Unless you're president of the United States, I suggest you steer clear of that approach. In fact, it's not a good idea even for the president, as it can breed resentment in the press corps. The short form answer I'm talking about, rather than being evasive, actually addresses the information sought, but not for very long. For example, the question is this: "Why is your company still using the X7 aircraft when everyone feels it's obsolete?" You don't want to talk about the X7; instead, you want to talk about a new freight service you're going to announce. Well, here's the first part of an answer: "**At Ynot Freight Express, we are convinced of the continued viability of the X7. We have been flying that particular aircraft for fifteen years.**" Notice, by the way, the branding right at the top of the answer. It was "At Ynot Freight Express" and not "We are convinced." The answer tells you who "we" are.

Step 2: Build a Bridge

Bridges need not be very elaborate. They are holding up nothing weightier than a transition. They are not meant to support your intentional message statements; they are just intended to get you to them. So the simpler and shorter the bridge, the better it is. "At Ynot Freight Express, we are convinced of the continued viability of the X7. We have been flying that particular aircraft for fifteen years. **In fact, we're so sure of its reliability . . .**" As bridges go, this one is pretty long. The bridge you build can be as short as a single word: "but," "however," "and." Or the bridge can be a few words that enable a transition: "on the other hand," "in addition to that," "as a matter of fact."

Step 3: State your IMS

"At Ynot Freight Express, we are convinced of the continued viability of the X7. We have been flying that particular aircraft for fifteen years, and we're so sure of its reliability **that we're using that plane to launch our exciting new freight service, which will save our customers $100 million a year without having a negative impact on our earnings. We call it a 'flying win-win.'**"

Step 4: Shut Up

If you stop talking after delivering your message, the chances are good the follow-up will be based on that message. If you bring the answer full circle, you're giving up control of the agenda. Pretend for a moment you're a reporter. What's your next question going to be about if you hear this answer: "At Ynot Freight Express, we are convinced of the continued viability of the X7. We have been flying that particular aircraft for fifteen years, and we're so sure of its reliability that we're using that plane to launch our exciting new freight service, which will save our customers $100 million a year without having a negative impact on our earnings. So of course we don't consider the aircraft obsolete." It's not going to be about the exciting freight service; it's going to be about the obsolescence of the aircraft. If the answer ended with the point about the money savings to the customers and the impact on Ynot's bottom line, chances are greater your next question would be about the freight service. "What is this new service?" or "How will this new service save your customers $100 million a year?" or "How can you cut your customers' costs by $100 million a year and not have a negative impact on your earnings?" Any one of these three questions keeps the interview in your IMS territory.

Bridging to an IMS from a question is counterintuitive for many of us. When we were in school we were taught to answer the question that was asked. Here, we're moving beyond the answer that we would have given in school to make a point we've crafted. In a scholastic setting—even in a social setting—this is bad manners. In an interview, it's part of your job.

The Interviewer's Top Seven Dirty Tricks

Can you use that bridge-building trick in a tough interview? Sure. In fact, many of the types of questions that on the surface appear to be probing and even hostile are easier to bridge than questions that are merely off-point and not asked in a challenging manner. The following are the top seven interviewer's dirty tricks and responses that show just how easy it is for a practiced bridge builder to use them to get to his IMSs.

Trick 1: Gross Misrepresentation

We've all seen this one. An interview subject gives an answer and the reporter interprets it for him, putting words in his mouth that he never intended to utter: "So what you're saying is this airplane, as near to retirement as it is, is going to be the backbone of a new service you're offering your customers?" How do you respond? By taking back control of your words: "No. [short form answer—shortest form answer, in fact] What I'm saying is [bridge] we are so convinced of the reliability of the aircraft that we're building our exciting new flying win-win service on it, a service that is going to save our customers $100 million a year." Watch "60 Minutes" or one of the other newsmagazine shows that specialize in investigative reporting and you'll see this "so what you're saying" technique used frequently. It is much less common on shows such as "Today," "The Early Show," or "Good Morning America."

"What you're saying" is usually followed by the reporter's taking what you've said beyond your original meaning. Of course, if the reporter is accurately characterizing what you're saying—which she may do because your expression of the concept wasn't totally clear and she wants you to take another crack at it—your response should be "Precisely. [short form answer] And, in fact [bridge], I can add . . . [cite additional IMS or reinforce your previous IMS]." I can recall a medical interview where, despite the reporter's extensive efforts to get a physician to use the word *miracle*, the doctor would not characterize a recovery that way. "So," the reporter said, "what you're saying is this isn't a miracle recovery?" "Exactly," the physician said. "It is an exceptional recovery, an unusual recovery. And what I'm saying is that if we carefully analyze how that recovery came about, it may afford us clues to how we should be treating this condition in other patients. That's the way science advances—by analyzing what we know and researching what we don't. It's no accident that the last six letters of 'research' spell 'search.'"

Trick 2: The Big Lie

The very premise of the question is false. Sometimes the reporter does this out of ignorance or shoddy research. And sometimes the reporter throws out a false premise to put her interview subject on the defensive. For example, "We know that the X7 aircraft is so obsolete that you are the only freight line in the country to use it." Never accept a false premise; correct it at once. Your correction is all the acknowledgment you need before building your bridge: "No, that's not the case. I know of several other airlines that use the plane. [short form answer] And, in fact [bridge], we are creating our exciting new flying win-win service around this aircraft. We call it a flying win-win because it's a service that will save our customers about $100 million every year." I can recall an interview about a nuclear-fueled vessel in which the interviewer demanded, "Isn't it true that there's enough plutonium in this to kill every man, woman, and child on the planet?" A great scare question if ever there was one. But the "fact" underlying the question was wrong, enabling the interview subject to say, "No, that's not the case at all. The amount of radioactive material in the vessel, spread worldwide, is less than normal background radiation in many parts of the world and certainly less than what you experience in a chest x-ray. But, even so, we have encased that material in a totally fail-safe environment." And he went on to deliver his IMS concerning safety precautions that had been designed into the vessel.

Trick 3: Assault with a Deadly Question

Mike Wallace is singularly adept at this one. The question is a hard-charging, accusatory, and sometimes inflammatory dig using loaded hot-button words: "Do you expect that the American people will believe an ancient aircraft like this is still viable and safe?" A deadly question is designed to elicit emotion as much as, if not more than, it is designed to elicit fact. In response, you must remain unemotional; if you do and the interviewer prods you, he's in danger of being seen as a bully. Calmly refute the charge, build a bridge, and move on to your IMS: "Why, yes, I expect that the American people will believe in the aircraft [short form answer] and [bridge] so do we at Ynot Freight Express because we're using that aircraft as the basis for our exciting new . . . [insert IMS here]" Doing a story on contaminated meat in supermarkets for "The Reasoner Report" at ABC News many years ago, a correspondent and I confronted a Connecticut State Health Department meat inspector with an accusation that he had taken bribes to look the other way when he found violations in a particular market. We had very specific charges against the man, but they came from a single witness and there was no hard evidence like photographs or documents to back up our witness's assertion. Our only hope to nail him was to get him to admit it or to deny it in a shifty, guilty way—or, better yet, to run away. The accusation was thrown at him in the form of an accusatory question delivered in the tone and style that TV prosecuting attorneys use. We were counting on him to begin sweating and shifting, stumbling and bumbling. But instead, he calmly and simply said, "No. That's not the case. Never happened. I would never do that." Needless to say, we didn't use the interview or the charge against him. Had he been media-trained, he might have gone on to add, "What I look for when protecting the public health is . . ."

Trick 4: The Dire Hypothetical

The reporter presents a disastrous scenario and invites you to comment on it: "What would happen if you discovered that the entire fleet of X7s had to be taken out of service immediately to have their engines and controls replaced?" Again, the short form answer is easy. First label the premise of the question: "That's a hypothetical proposition that has no basis in fact or historical record. [short form answer] A much more likely scenario [bridge] is that these planes will continue to serve our customers well as we announce our exciting new . . . [insert IMS here]"

Trick 5: The Interruption

Rather than waiting for you to finish a statement, the reporter jumps in, stopping you cold and throwing another question at you. This happens mostly in antagonistic broadcast interviews where the reporter is playing the role of tough guy with you. The best way to turn this rude technique to your advantage is to highlight the fact that the reporter is deploying it. Say, "Well, I was about to say . . ." and move on to an IMS. Unspoken in your response—but clear to viewers and listeners—is the phrase "before you so rudely interrupted me." If he persists, you may want to call attention directly to it: "You know, Peter, a number of times you've interrupted me before I could finish my thought. What I'd like people to know is . . ." and insert an IMS right there. Calling attention to his rudeness will usually cure it. Most reporters don't want to appear to be boors. It is unusual for print reporters to employ this trick; there is nothing in it for them, whereas a broadcast journalist gets to appear tough and uncompromising when he does it.

Trick 6: The Filibuster

Some reporters love the sound of their own voices so much—or think they know so much—that they hog *your* interview and won't shut up. I have found that to be true especially when the reporter is a specialist who is anxious to show off how much he knows. Often his questions may be an occasional "Would you agree?" or "Don't you agree?" after he's made a speech. While the temptation may be for you to sit quietly by while the reporter gives you a pass by asking very few questions, you would miss an opportunity to insert your IMSs if you let him get away with it. What to do? Well, when he throws one of those "Would you agree?" questions at you, say, "Yes. [short form answer] As a matter of fact [bridge], . . ." and launch into your IMS. If you disagree, say, "No. [short form answer] In point of fact [bridge], . . ." and deliver an IMS. Now if he persists in these filibusters and doesn't even bother to ask you to agree or disagree with him, it's incumbent on you to find an opening and jump in. Listen carefully and when he makes a point you agree with (or disagree with), jump in, express your agreement or disagreement, and bridge to an IMS. If you have to interrupt him while he's speaking, do it when he's made a point with which you agree so you won't sound *quite* so rude. In terms of timing, jump in when he pauses to draw a breath; even the most enthusiastic filibusterer must breathe. While it is usually a good idea to deliver no more than one IMS in a single answer, in this instance make an exception to that rule. In fact, forget the KISS injunction, too. You fight fire with fire and a filibuster with a filibuster. It may be the only way you'll be able to work in any of your IMSs. Early in my television career I worked with a reporter who had a specialty beat and fancied himself more expert in his particular area of expertise than most of the people he interviewed. He was, in fact, extremely knowledgeable and in general was far better able to express the complex ideas of his area of expertise than many of the people he interviewed. Ideally, he wanted to interview only himself, but the management at the network news division where we worked would not have permitted that and audiences might have found it bizarre, to say the least. Since he couldn't interview himself, he was given to making long pronouncements and then asking his interview subjects, "Don't you agree?" After a while some of them were reduced to just nodding assent. It made my life hell when I got back to the editing suite and had to try to cut a soundbite out of the interview. The more media savvy would say, "Yes, I agree," and then express the same point in their own words.

Trick 7: The Pregnant Pause

Earlier I told you to take advantage of a pause in a friendly interview; when a reporter is searching his prepared questions for the next one to ask, I advised, jump in with an IMS. Hostile reporters use pauses, too, but not to find their next question. They use them as an invitation for you to expand on answers you've already given—invitations to go where you may not want to go. I first became aware of this practice when Harry Reasoner appeared on the "David Frost Show." At the time, British interviewer Frost had talk shows on both sides of the Atlantic and commuted by Concorde from London to New York a couple times a week. Frost eventually gave up that exhausting schedule and concentrated on his British career, which is why we rarely see him in this country anymore. Harry and I had been on a weeklong promotional tour for ABC News right after he was hired to anchor the nightly network newscast. Our last stop was the Frost show in New York. Having listened to Harry give interviews for a week, I had heard all of his quip-filled, clever answers to the predictable questions. But when he delivered one of these to Frost, the Briton nodded, looked at Reasoner, and said nothing. Whereupon Reasoner, feeling the weight of the silence, jumped in and added to his stock answer. Frost did this several times during the interview. When we left the studio, Harry said to me, "Frost is a master of the pregnant pause. He got more out of me than any of the other interviewers this week." So if your interviewer's pause is motivated by his search for his next question, jump in. But if the pause is motivated by his desire for you to go up the gallows steps and stick your head in his noose, don't take advantage of the silence. Usually, it's easy to tell the difference: the question-searching pause is characterized by the reporter looking at his notes; the pregnant pause is characterized by the reporter looking you in the eye.

In all the instances I've cited, it's really important that you avoid repeating any negative phrases or words in the question. In a broadcast interview, if you repeat the negative words, the audience will hear the loaded words twice, once in the reporter's question and a second time in your answer, as in this example: "Isn't this nuclear plant just a Chernobyl disaster waiting to happen?" "Why no, it's not a Chernobyl disaster waiting to happen at all. . . ." You don't want to be adding emphasis to the negative words, so don't allow yourself to be lured into repeating them. In a print interview, it takes very little for a skilled writer to craft a direct quote from your use of the negative words you've repeated, even if you've repeated them in refutation. Just imagine you're the company spokesperson in this line from a hypothetical newspaper story: " 'This program is not a Chernobyl disaster waiting to happen,' the company spokesperson said." The "Chernobyl disaster waiting to happen" was in the question the reporter did not print in his story. But you did him the favor of repeating it in your answer, and the quote looks pretty bad even though it is a refutation. Just today I read a story in the *Los Angeles Times* quoting the spokesperson for an arts center that was having trouble raising money for an addition. The center had embarked on a new fund-raising scheme, and the spokesperson was quoted as saying, "This is not a desperation move." As an experienced reporter, it was obvious to me that the phrase "desperation move" was contained in the question. By repeating it in his answer, the spokesperson gave the reporter those dramatic words in a direct quote. Sometimes an interview subject doesn't even need the introduction of negative words in a question. During the Watergate scandal, President Nixon told a news conference, "I'm not a crook." Well, no one had asked him if he was a crook. He read that unspoken negative word into a question he had been asked and used it in his answer. As Shakespeare wrote in *Hamlet*, "The lady doth protest too much, methinks." Don't refute what isn't charged, and don't indict yourself by repeating the negative in a question.

Eleven Rules for Acing an Interview

There are eleven rules you need to follow in order to prepare for and ace a tough or hostile interview. It's a good idea, by the way, to follow these rules for all interviews, because, as noted earlier, even a kindly reporter can turn tough if the situation warrants or if she perceives that it's necessary to adopt that tone to get her story.

Rule 1: Play Reporter

Use worksheet 4 ("Worst Questions in the World") in the Appendix to write down the hard questions you might get in an interview. If you don't write down and study the questions that keep you up nights, you won't be prepared when they are thrown at you. Remember Merlis's

Law of Interviews: anyone unprepared for tough questions will be asked tough questions. You might say that those who are unprepared are magnets for tough questions.

Rule 2: Answer the Tough Questions

It does you no good to anticipate those tough questions if you don't also prepare your answers. Look at each question and decide which of your IMSs you might be able to work into a response without creating segue whiplash for the reporter. As an exercise, pair IMSs with individual tough questions. Just because you're prepared with answers to tough questions, there's no reason to invite them. If they come, use your prepared answers. If they don't come, you're that much further ahead. A dramatic example of soliciting tough questions was the December 27, 2002, news conference by the company Clonaid, which claimed it was the first to clone a human being. The CEO of the company, which has ties to a religious cult, said at the conference, "The baby is very healthy. She is fine, she is doing fine. The parents are happy. I hope that you remember them when you talk about this baby, not like a monster, like the result of something that is disgusting." This one ranks with Richard Nixon's "I'm not a crook."

Rule 3: Rehearse Tough Questions

Have someone ask you those tough questions and videotape the session. Tell your inquisitor to be merciless with you. When you screen your tape, grade yourself on how well you did in building bridges to your messages. Even if you did well the first time, repeat the exercise. You want to get almost comfortable under withering questions. Almost comfortable, but not totally comfortable. You never want to be so comfortable in an interview that you forget you are performing and not just having a chat with a buddy.

Rule 4: Tape the Interview

Your best defense against being misquoted in print or against having your answer A paired with her question B in a broadcast story is to tape-record your interview. And let the reporter know you are tape-recording it. You'll want to review the tape immediately after the interview to make sure you didn't misspeak. If you find that you did, call the reporter at once, tell her you gave her an incorrect fact or expressed yourself incorrectly in one of your answers during the interview, and supply the correct answer. (Record this conversation, too. It is your only "evidence" that you corrected your error.) In thirteen states and the Commonwealth of Puerto Rico, laws require that you tell all parties to a conversation or phone call they are being recorded; the other states and the federal government permit unannounced recording of conversations and phone calls.[1] But it is a good policy from both ethical and practical points of view to announce that you are recording the interview even if your state permits clandestine recordings. Ethically, you are putting all your cards on the table. Practically, you are alerting the reporter that he'd better represent your answers accurately. Not too long ago I saw a tape of a client's interview with an investigative reporter. Having been an investigative producer myself, I saw a number of opportunities where a less-than-totally-ethical reporter might have been able to twist and tilt the client's words to work against him. In this case, it didn't happen, because the reporter was ethical. I can't say for a certainty that the knowledge my client was recording the interview contributed to the reporter's ethics, but it could not have hurt.

Rule 5: Bring a Witness

In addition to recording the interview, you should have a witness on hand. It helps to have a knowledgeable colleague, whether from your department or your public relations staff, sitting in on the interview. Occasionally, under the pressure of the moment, you might misspeak, give an incorrect fact or figure, or get a name wrong. The less-pressured colleague can interject and offer you the correct information. Obviously, this doesn't work in a live broadcast interview, but in all other inter-

---

1. The thirteen states that require all parties to a conversation to be aware that you are taping are California, Connecticut, Delaware, Florida, Illinois, Maryland, Massachusetts, Michigan, Montana, Nevada, New Hampshire, Pennsylvania, and Washington. There is no federal requirement for informing all parties that you are recording a conversation.

views it can be helpful. The colleague should not interrupt you mid-sentence to correct you. She should wait until you've finished your answer at the very least, and, in the case of a taped broadcast interview, she should wait until the camera has stopped recording before speaking up, so that her correction doesn't became a part of the on-air story.

Rule 6: Remain Calm

In broadcast interviews especially, sometimes the drama of having a flustered or angry interview subject is more important than having the facts of a story. (More on that in Chapters 6 and 7.) You can remain in control of the agenda only if you remain unemotional. By unemotional, I don't mean being a flatliner wearing a toe tag on a hospital gurney. I mean avoiding displays of anger or guilty nervousness. Even impatience, as former vice president Al Gore can attest, is perceived as a negative emotion by television viewers. While the challenge is especially acute in broadcast interviews, even print interviewers can use your emotions if you display them. "His faced flushed with anger and his voice rising, Mr. X defended Ynot Corporation against . . ." Just today I read an article in *New York Magazine* about Connecticut senator Joe Lieberman that included a quote from his wife, Hadassah. The writer quoted Mrs. Lieberman's words and at the end of the quote did not write "she said," but rather, "she snapped." Those loaded words betrayed Hadassah Lieberman's attitude toward the question. The better prepared you are with IMSs, with answers to anticipated tough questions, and with bridges to your IMSs, the easier it will be for you to remain calm and in control and the less "snapping" you'll do.

Rule 7: Don't Go off the Record

Anything you say to a reporter can be used. It might be paraphrased, but the facts could wind up in print or on the air. Also, your confidence might not be respected. You might think you've said something off the record, but the reporter might think it's on the record—and once he acts on his understanding, it *is* on the record. Even a reporter who promises to keep something you've told him off the record might be pressured by his superiors to put it on the record or in the story in a way it can be traced to you. When I was executive producer of "Good Morning America," the television press was always out to skewer David Hartman, the show's host. David was reputed to be a tough, even unreasonable, taskmaster for the staff, and that was the sort of story the press loved—nice guy on camera, monster behind the scenes. On numerous occasions, television columnists, many of them old friends of mine from my days as a publicist for ABC News, would offer me the opportunity to comment off the record on the supposed dual David Hartmans. Whether the story was true or not, what was in it for me or for the show if negative stories about the host of the show saw the light of print? We were number one in the morning ratings in those days, convincingly trouncing "Today" week in and week out, and if people became disaffected because they read negative stories about David and if they stopped watching the show, I was going to be one of the first sacrificial lambs. Even if the negative buzz had been true and even if I had harbored grudges against Hartman, I stood to gain nothing by sharing this with the press. I consistently declined opportunities to go off the record about David. I did, on a number of occasions, exercise the one exception to the "off-the-record" rule, and you can, too: state in an off-the-record comment something you would just as willingly say on the record. "Off the record," a reporter would urge me, seeking some juicy story about Hartman's off-camera persona. "Off the record," I would say, "David is the hardest-working member of the staff, and he demands far more of himself than he demands of any of us." My "off the record" was really a way of putting an on-the-record statement in boldface.

Rule 8: Don't Supply Information Not for Attribution

A favorite trick of government and some private sector officials is to give reporters information on a not-for-attribution basis, as in, "A high-level official of the Ynot Corporation told the *Daily Bugle* that . . ." It's usually pretty easy to trace the source of the quote. So if you're giving a statement not for attribution in order to keep out of the whistle-blower's spotlight, don't do it—you'll be found out. It doesn't take a very sophisticated reader to figure out who the speaker is in most stories. And in some formats, the speaker is a virtual given. For example, the "high-level State Department official traveling with the secretary of state" who gives all those frank assessments of foreign leaders is actually the secretary of state.

Rule 9: Don't Ever Answer a Question with "No Comment"

A "no comment" in an interview is like taking the Fifth Amendment in a congressional hearing or in court. True, you're within your constitutional rights to avoid self-incrimination, but to the public, invoking the Fifth looks incriminating. The perception is that the person who takes the Fifth Amendment has something to hide. Similarly, "no comment" looks evasive, largely because it is evasive. If you can't comment, you can use that to begin building a bridge to an IMS. Here's how to do it: First, tell the reporter why you can't comment. It may be that the question seeks information involving active litigation, and either company policy or a judicial admonition prevents you from commenting. It may be that the question is about a matter outside your area of expertise or authority. Or it may be that the answer would reveal proprietary information and put your company at a competitive disadvantage. By announcing why you can't address the question, you've actually given the short form answer that sets you up to build the bridge to your IMS. Without using the loaded phrase "no comment," here's how it works: "I really can't answer that because it's a matter that's in active litigation and the judge has imposed a gag order. [short form answer]" (Or, if there is no judicial admonition against discussing the case, "Company policy prohibits talking about matters that are in litigation.") "But [bridge] what I can tell you is . . . [insert IMS here]" Then you shut up! Don't go full circle and finish your answer saying something like, "And that's why I can't address your question." Looking back at the start of the statement, notice that I substituted "can't answer" for "can't comment." Another alternative is, "I really can't address that."

Rule 10: Don't Guess

Guessing at an answer is dangerous; you could be wrong. But if you don't know an answer, use that lack of knowledge as a short form answer: "I don't know. I can find out for you and get back to you on it. [short form answer] But what I do know [bridge] is that . . . [insert IMS]" Don't be bullied into guessing. Following your initial answer, a prosecutorial reporter might thunder, "You don't know? You don't know? How can you not know? Isn't it your job to know?" Don't let him shake you up so much that you are reduced to guessing. "That's right. As I said, I'll find out and get that for you. What I do know is . . ." and move on to a second IMS. If he keeps at it, he could well enable every one of your IMSs. He'll realize this in short order and move on.

Rule 11: Rephrase the Question

Earlier we talked about how an interviewer will sometimes put words in your mouth. That tactic works both ways. You can put words in her mouth by starting your answer to her question this way: "You're asking me if . . ." This allows you to restate the question more to your liking. Obviously, this doesn't work with a very simple and direct question like, "How long will it take to clean up the toxic spill in your factory's backyard?" And your restatement has to have more than a passing similarity to the original question. For instance, you can't say, "What you're asking me is how effective our affirmative action policy has been . . . ," if the original question was, "Were you here when the chemical spill polluted the groundwater?"

Be Specific

The media and their audiences love specifics. Anytime you can give a case history or a concrete example of a general concept, you are communicating effectively.

A good rule of thumb is that the general concept can be inferred from the specific, but the specific cannot be inferred from the general. You can use specifics introducing or concluding general statements. I prefer them as supporting proof of an IMS and coming at the end because they invite favorable comment from the reporter or they give him a cue for his next question. It's not enough to say, for instance, "The space program has given society lots of technological and scientific advances." The reader of the newspaper or the viewer of the TV broadcast containing that quote is also listening to that universal radio station WSIC. If your quote ends there, he will mentally ask you, "Oh yeah, like what?" You need to fill in that blank. Tell him the specifics that back up the generalized statement. For instance, "The space program has given society lots of technological and scientific advances. Walk into the radiology department of any modern hospital and you will see diagnostic tools such as MRIs that were developed as an outgrowth of technology created for the space program." Now he knows why he should care; technology created for the space program has been adapted to create machines that may one day save his life. The specific brings home the intentional message statement.

A specific need not be an itemized list, although that helps. In January 2003, when two U.S. Air Force reservists were threatened with court martial in connection with a mistaken bombing in Afghanistan that killed four Canadian soldiers, their first line of defense was that their judgment had been clouded because they had taken Air Force–issued amphetamines, or "go pills," which pilots could use to stay alert during long missions. That practice came under media scrutiny, and the Air Force had a pilot-surgeon explain the use of the pills to the media. He might have said simply, "These pills save lives by keeping pilots alert." But the officer, Colonel Peter Demitry, was ready with what I would call a generalized specific and a few grabbers. Here's some of what he said, speaking of the low-dosage amphetamine tablets issued to pilots. I've put the specific in boldface and the grabbers in italic. "It is the *gold standard* for antifatigue. We know that fatigue in aviation kills. *We have **the smoking holes, the irreplaceable loss of life**. This is a *life-and-death insurance* policy that saves lives." I put his specific in boldface and italic because his specific is such a good word picture that it qualifies as a grabber as well. My only criticism of Colonel Demitry's soundbite is the very first word: "It." His statement would have been more specific and broadcast-compatible had he said, "The low-dose energizing amphetamines we issue to pilots are the *gold standard* for antifatigue. We know that fatigue in aviation kills. *We have **the smok-***

ing holes, the irreplaceable loss of life. This is a *life-and-death insurance* policy that saves lives."

The Postinterview Cooldown

I have concluded interviews and seen the subject leap up out of his seat and begin sprinting from the room, only to be halted by the microphone cord attached to his tie. You, too, may feel like fleeing immediately after your interview, even if it was conducted in your own office, but resist this urge. The postinterview cooldown is just as important as the preinterview warm-up.

In the cooldown, as in the warm-up, you shouldn't say anything to the reporter you don't want the whole world to hear. Also, you can use the cooldown (as you used the warm-up) to plant additional ideas.

For example, don't say, "Gee, I'm so glad you didn't ask me about XYZ; I was really afraid of that one." That injunction may sound like a given to you, but a number of interview subjects have expressed just that sentiment to me over the years using a variety of phrases. My journalistic instinct on hearing this sort of comment is then to probe deeper and get them to open up and offer answers to previously unasked questions. I've even had crews stop packing their camera gear, reset their lights, and begin shooting after an interview subject let slip a similar postinterview line.

Use the cooldown to suggest additional resources to the reporter—resources that back up your point of view. "You know, if you're interested in learning more about this, I'd suggest speaking to Dr. Hackley. He's done a lot of research in the field." Leave unspoken, "And he agrees with me completely." Or, if you realize that you've failed to get one of your key messages into the interview, bring it up during the cooldown. The reporter may not go for the bait, but you've nothing to lose by dangling it. In a print interview, that additional message may be seamlessly integrated into the story and the reader won't even know it was an afterthought. In a broadcast story, the reporter might use the information by saying on camera to the viewers, "Mr. XYZ also told me that Ynot

Corporation is contemplating doubling its dividend next quarter." We've all seen this on TV—further information that was not included in the taped interview but was added by the reporter. Chances are these points were learned by the reporter in the cooldown after the lights were off and the camera was packed up.

The Good Guest

In my newspaper years, there were a number of people I would go back to time after time for comments on stories. They were the print equivalent of television's good guests. A good guest or good interview is someone who makes the reporter's job easier by being prepared, speaking clearly and comprehensibly, and giving good, pithy, even entertaining quotes.

Most good guests are thought-provoking. They may accomplish this through a deft use of language, introduction of new and fresh information, or expression of new and fresh viewpoints on information in general circulation. Or they may get our attention by throwing the biggest verbal bricks through the biggest plate-glass windows. Think Jesse Jackson on the Left and Newt Gingrich on the Right; both convey their points of view through the skillful wielding of entertainingly outrageous soundbites. They delight their core constituencies and infuriate their core opponents. By using hot-button words and provocative phrases, they virtually force those in the middle to make a choice—or at least to think about their messages. Whether you are courting or skirting controversy, you can be a good guest if you are well prepared, use precise language and easily grasped specific examples or case histories, and sprinkle your interviews with trenchant grabbers.

Don't Do Lunch

A meal is a meal and an interview is an interview, and the two should not be mixed. There are just too many distractions at a mealtime interview. It's virtually guaranteed that a waiter will bring a dish just as you're beginning to unleash one of your best grabbers. Also, if the food is good, valuable time will be spent praising it. And if the food is bad, valuable time will be spent complaining about it. Restaurants are full of clatter and chatter, all of which will serve to distract from your primary reason for doing the interview. In the world of broadcasting, you may find yourself trying to talk with your mouth full—which is never attractive. In a print interview, the reporter may take the space in her article to describe the meal and the dining room when you really want her to spend every bit of space discussing your ideas and message points. Finally, if you spill a drink, choke on a forkful of steak, or drop your butter knife on your lap, the mishap could end up in the article, making you look clumsy, careless, or ill-mannered. Even if the reporter offers to pay for the meal—and that will be the day!—don't do it. Similarly, an interview over cocktails is an invitation to disaster for obvious and subtle reasons. Even if the drink you have with a reporter is non-alcoholic or even if the alcoholic drink you have doesn't affect your performance, she can still write, with perfect accuracy, "Interviewed over drinks, Mr. Fields said . . ." And if an alcoholic drink consumed during an interview does affect you, the reporter is likely to mention it in her article.

The tips in this chapter pertain to all interviews in all media. Some additional, unique skills should be mastered in order for you to be most effective in broadcast encounters. It won't hurt to employ these specific skills in print interviews as well. Communicating with all media using the broadcast skill set will make you a livelier, more interesting, more quoted interviewee. You can read more on television's unique demands in the next chapter.

CHAPTER 5

CATERING TO THE ONE-EYED BEAST:
TELEVISION APPEARANCES

If you are going to appear on television, you must watch television. I don't mean "NYPD Blue" or "Scrubs," although they're fun to watch. I mean information programming, news programming, interview programming, and especially programming on which you're likely to appear because watching the program lets you know what to expect when it's your turn to be interviewed.

Is the show live and unedited ("Larry King Live," "Nightline," "Meet the Press," "Good Morning America") or taped and edited ("60 Minutes," "Dateline NBC," "20/20")? Is the show serious or flippant? Are guests interviewed singly or are they pitted against each other in a shoutfest? (See Chapter 7 on how to win a shoutfest.) Does the host have a political or social agenda (John Stossel, Chris Matthews) or is the host journalistic (Ted Koppel, Stone Phillips, Paula Zahn)? Does the host listen to answers or just read a list of prepared questions and never follow up? Is the host polite (Larry King) or tough to the point of being hostile (Mike Wallace)? Are you seated or standing? Is everyone dressed casually or formally? Are interviews long or short? If it's an edited show, are the soundbites generally lengthy and substantive or brief and vapid?

Moreover, by watching, you'll be able to ascertain who the viewer is and what he or she wants to hear about. You'll speak differently to an audience of businesspeople (CNBC) than to a general audience ("The Today Show"). You can speak at greater length on some live interview shows ("Larry King Live") than you can on my alma mater, "Good

Morning America." Your audience may be composed of sophisticated and knowledgeable news junkies ("The NewsHour with Jim Lehrer") or it may be more frivolous ("Live with Regis and Kelly"). The more familiar you are with the show, the talent, and the format, the more at ease you'll be and the better prepared to unleash your good IMSs.

The Nature of the Beast

Early in my television career I worked for an executive producer who was fond of proclaiming, "Television is a visual medium," and who then "watched" the first cut of any report with his eyes closed. He did that so he could get the full essence of the written script and spoken soundbites. In those days, television news reports were shot on film, and the picture and soundtracks were separate. Once, as a gag, I had the editor play a rough cut for Mr. Visual without running the picture. The report ran its full four or five minutes, the screen blank, the soundtrack at normal level. When the piece ended, the executive producer said, "That was pretty good; let's see it again." Since it was his practice to actually watch the second time through, the editor ran the picture as well as the track.

Notwithstanding the editor's and my juvenile bit of insubordination, television is much more heavily dependent on visuals than any other medium. And some stories are almost totally picture-driven.

Several years ago, the magazine *Consumer Reports* gave an unsatisfactory rating to an imported sport utility vehicle because the *Consumer Reports* engineers had gotten their test vehicle to tip over in a high-speed maneuver. Well, it was an interesting story to hear on the radio or read in a newspaper, but it was a riveting story to see on television. The *Consumer Reports*–supplied tape showed the vehicle speeding into a curve and tipping violently, with its wheels lifting off the pavement. (A training wheel–like device kept the SUV from actually going over on its side.) This story had such a strong visual impact that it was impossible for the manufacturer to counter it with mere words. Instead, the manufacturer had to stage and film its own test of the vehicle.

When you are preparing for a television interview, you must think about whether there are visuals—tape, stills, animation, even drawings—that will help you make your points. In the SUV case, the best defense was not a corporate engineer saying the *Consumer Reports* test was biased, but the tape of the test the manufacturer had another laboratory conduct, which they claimed refuted the *Consumer Reports* findings. Television loves visuals, so think visually. The viewers, unlike my old executive producer, will be watching as well as listening, and whatever images you can produce to buttress what you are saying will help immeasurably.

Why do presidents enhance their major addresses with charts and graphs? Why do NASA spokespersons almost always have model spacecraft on the table or desk before them and a handout tape of a mission animation when they do an interview? Why do actors plugging a film on a talk show bring clips or outtakes of the movie? Because these simple aids add visual interest to the coverage and make stories come alive on television. If you think visually, you will ask yourself what you can offer the television reporter by way of visuals to enhance and illustrate your IMSs. Film, tape, animation, stills, graphs, charts, maps—all can make for a much more interesting television story than just a talking head.

How to Look Good on TV

If I say appearances count on television, I don't want to give the impression, as early practitioners of media training did, that appearances are all that count. Content counts, too. An energetic, attractive spokesperson who says nothing is delivering no message save that she is energetic and attractive.

That said, appearance has unique impact in television. The greatest single object lesson in how much appearance counts in the medium dates back to the early days of black-and-white broadcasting. In the very first televised presidential debate in 1960, then-senator Richard M. Nixon eschewed makeup, sweated profusely—as was his wont throughout his career—and, not knowing where to look, glanced nervously from side to side. Conversely, then-senator John F. Kennedy—guided by instinct or coaching or both—kept his gaze fixed on his questioners, used an orator's hand gestures to help him make his points, and seemed tanned and fit, probably thanks to Max Factor TV makeup. The result: people who watched the debate awarded Kennedy a "win."

But the debate was simulcast on radio, and listeners, who had no visual clues to go by and could judge only by the content of what was said, thought the debate was more like a draw, with Nixon delivering substantive points in his deep, resonant voice. The difference was cosmetic; on radio it didn't matter, while on television it was the line between winning and losing. While this may be a sad comment on the state of democracy in the age of television, it is the fact of the matter. Recall former vice president Al Gore during his campaign against George W. Bush for the presidency. He rolled his eyes and shook his head in condescending impatience at Bush during their first debate, and the public reacted negatively. If you ignore the cosmetic side of television, thinking that it's not a substantive part of your appearance, you'll likely end up disappointed with the way the audience receives your message.

Despite the importance of the cosmetic side, looking good is not enough on television; it won't overcome an absence of substance. But without paying eye service to the cosmetic demands of the medium, it is hard to convey intentional message statements to viewers. Think of the appearance requirements of television as the visual equivalent of a clear writing style. In print, dense, garbled sentences don't convey your ideas very well. You strive for clarity in written communication; you don't want the writing to get in the way of your thoughts. On television, your appearance and attitude are your visual writing style.

Here, then, are eight simple wardrobe, appearance, and performance rules for television:

1. Dress right.
2. Sit right.
3. Stand right.
4. Move right.

5. Emote right.
6. Look right.
7. Talk right.
8. Leave right.

Dress Right

As president, Richard Nixon hosted my old ABC News colleague Gary Herman and his camera crew at his Western White House in San Clemente. To humanize his image, Nixon took his wife, Pat, for an on-camera walk along the beach. Characteristically, Nixon wore a dark business suit, a tie, and lace-up black wing-tip shoes. Had he been in a pair of Bermuda shorts and barefoot, the scene would have looked natural and charming instead of staged and awkward. As ridiculous as the suit-on-the-beach stroll looked, it got worse when a particularly high wave washed up on shore and the president did a little dance in a futile attempt to avoid getting his wing-tips soaked. ABC News did Nixon the favor of not airing that particular bit of film; walking down a beach in a business suit was odd enough without the water-dodging jig the president performed.

It ought to be self-evident that a suit on a beach is as out of place as a pair of swim trunks in an office. What do you wear for television? If business attire is correct for the occasion or for your position, men should wear a dark blue or gray suit without a pattern, and women a suit or daytime dress with the same color considerations. Avoid brown. President Ronald Reagan was partial to a brown suit, which under certain lighting conditions looked reddish on TV. Wear a solid color shirt or blouse—pale blue is best—and avoid bright colors, striped shirts, ties, and scarves. Also, wear lightweight clothing. Television lighting has come a long way since Richard Nixon poured sweat in 1960, and studios are much cooler than they once were. But TV lights are bright and they do generate heat, so dress accordingly.

Men should wear over-the-calf socks so we don't see a slash of exposed flesh between trouser cuff and sock top. Women should avoid overly short skirts; oftentimes you will be sitting on a low chair—with all the hazards that represents. Jewelry should be minimal—avoid any dangling necklaces that might hit your microphone. Also, if you're wearing the rock of Gibraltar on your finger, on your wrist, or around your neck, the chances are pretty good you're not going to connect with the average woman out there who could feed her family for a decade on what you spent for the stone. The same goes for men's bejeweled pinkie rings and diamond-encrusted wristwatches.

If business attire is not appropriate, you should still be dressed neatly, in subdued colors and no stripes. Obviously, if you are the fire boss fighting a blaze in a national forest, neatness does not matter. Avoid shirts and jackets with a lot of printing on them; you want the viewers to be watching you, not trying to read your clothing. The only exception to that rule is your own company's or organization's logo. Then it is merely reinforcing your on-screen identification. More businesses and organizations are requiring employees to wear ID tags or badges. You'll want to remove these before an interview; they can create distracting reflections, and more than a few viewers will try to read them while you're talking.

Sit Right

Your mother was right: sit up straight in your chair. If you've watched interviews with sullen young stars of the music and acting worlds, you know why. They sit on their necks, legs splayed in a wide V, inviting your attention to their crotches instead of their faces.

Sit the way the Victorians did, perched on the forward two-thirds of the chair, your back not even touching the seatback. In fact, you might want to lean in slightly toward the interviewer. Your body language will be saying you are eager to talk with him, and the viewer assumes you are just as eager to communicate with her, too. Leaning back sends the opposite body language signal—you are physically retreating from the interviewer and from the viewer.

And by all means, don't fidget. Once again, Mom was right. A lot of us channel our nervous energy through our legs. We bounce our knees or drum our foot or—when we are in a chair that swivels—we do a seated version of the old rock-and-roll dance favorite, the twist. You can guess the kind of message this sends to your viewers. If you plant your feet solidly on the floor, imagining your heels glued to the deck, then it is nearly impossible to drum feet, bounce knees, or swivel your chair.

Stand Right

Standing interviews tend to be shorter than seated interviews, probably because the interviewer is as uncomfortable standing up as you are. When doing a standing interview, stand up straight; don't slump and never lock your knees, as the lack of blood circulation could cause you to pass out—not an effective way to convey your message.

Stand with your feet about shoulder width apart. This will keep you from rocking from side to side. Keep your hands out of your pockets and avoid clutching them protectively over your crotch in what I call the CUP (for cover up privates) position. In March of 2003 former president Bill Clinton and former senator Bob Dole appeared on the "CBS Morning Show" to announce their debut as commentators on "60 Minutes." Side by side, the former senator, who made commercials for Viagra, and the former president, whose administration was almost brought down by a sex scandal, both adopted the CUP pose for much of their interview with Harry Smith.

Move Right

Be expressive, talk with your head, shoulders, and hands, and give your conversation energy and animation.

Why do singers use hand gestures? Why do actors use their hands when delivering dialogue? For three excellent reasons:

1. **Using your hands helps you make a point.** When a singer belts out a lyric about love, she often clutches her hands to her heart and then thrusts them wide. The gestures are helping her tell the story of the song. Similarly, when you say, "This is the biggest thing that's ever happened to our company," and you spread your arms in a modified "soooo big" gesture, you're reinforcing the point you're making. Additionally, gestures can help you remember. If I were on television right now, telling the viewer why it's important to use

hand gestures, I would demonstrate the three points by ticking them off on my fingers. Not only do I reinforce the fact that there are three points, but I also remind *myself* that there are three points to be described.

2. **Gestures attract attention; they make you look active.** Let's hark back to that 1960 presidential debate. Kennedy dramatized his points with very deliberate, almost karate-chop hand gestures. Nixon, for the most part, let his hands rest on the lectern in front of him. Kennedy was interesting to look at—in a positive sense. What was most interesting in Nixon's appearance was his unfortunate and unrelenting sweat.

3. **Gestures help energize your voice.** Again, look at singers—they gesture not only to illustrate their songs but also to help them throw their voices to the last row of the highest balcony. For the interview subject, gestures have the added benefit of allowing you to burn off nervous energy and turn that nervousness into something productive.

A cautionary note: if hand gestures are totally foreign to your nature, skip them. Forcing yourself to gesticulate unnaturally will divert important mental energy away from your intentional message statements. If you cannot gesture with ease, you are going to look like some sort of puppet when you force yourself to do it.

Emote Right

Once, I was producing an interview with a spokesman for an automobile company. What he was saying was serious, though the way he was saying it was not. Even giving grim economic news, he had an idiot's grin smeared across his face and looked like a commercial for cosmetic dentistry. Finally, I did him the favor of stopping the tape and asking him why, when he was dealing with a negative story, he looked so happy.

"My media trainer told me I should always smile. It makes me look friendly," he explained. And, I thought, it also makes you look totally unconcerned about what you're saying. I suggested that "concerned" was more important than "friendly" in this case, and he stopped grinning.

I wasn't in the room when he underwent media training, so I can't testify about whether or not his recollection of his lesson was accurate. Regardless, the moral of this story is to stop grinning like a Halloween jack-o'-lantern. Your expression should be appropriate to what you are saying. Go with your gut instincts on facial expressions; you know a big bright smile doesn't mesh with grim news, and a mournful look totally defeats a positive statement.

Look Right

You'll recall that candidate Richard Nixon had a tough time deciding where to look when he engaged John Kennedy in that first presidential debate. Consequently, he looked from side to side and forever earned the reputation for being shifty-eyed. It was such an enduring image that during the mad merchandising orgy that accompanied the Watergate scandal, a company put out a "Tricky Dick" watch adorned with a cartoon Nixon whose eyes shifted back and forth to tick off the seconds. Trust me, there are better ways of securing your fifteen minutes of fame than being some guy's timepiece.

Where do you look if your interviewer has one of those hypnotic stares or, more commonly, is not looking at you but down in her lap where her list of prepared questions is resting? For the former condition, look at a spot on her forehead just above the eyes. For the latter, look at where her eyes would be if she were looking at you. Staring into someone else's lap is never a good idea on television.

Normally, I tell clients never to look in the camera unless they are doing a remote interview—in other words, the interviewer is not in the room with them, but across town or across the country. In that case, the lens of the camera should be treated as if it were the interviewer's eye.

There is another exception to this rule of not engaging the camera. It needs to be used sparingly and judiciously and only by certain spokespersons. In general, you look into the lens of the camera during a face-to-face interview only when you want to share a moment with viewers directly. Pulling your attention away from the interview and staring down the barrel of the lens can be extremely jarring and should be done with great care and never more than once during an interview. And, if you're going to do it, then do it. Don't start talking toward the lens and then turn back to your interrogator before you finish the thought; that destroys the effect. Spokespersons who undertake the direct-to-viewer approach should be the most practiced and confident. Be forewarned: this is no trick for a novice.

Talk Right

As indicated in Chapter 3, talking to the media is different from talking to your colleagues. You must banish jargon and write a verbal headline for your intentional message statement—in other words, lead with your strongest stuff. You also need to keep it short and simple and use grabbers to capture a viewer's or reader's attention. For television, you'll also want to inject some energy into your voice; if you don't sound interested in what you're talking about, the viewer won't be interested either. Energy, by the way, is not speed. You don't want to talk so fast that you outpace your viewers' ability to follow your ideas. And you need to know when to stop talking.

Talk Right in the Warm-Up

In the last chapter, we covered the warm-up phase gaffe of saying to your interviewer—or anyone who might pass it on to your interviewer—"Gosh, I hope you aren't going to ask me about XYZ." Saying something like that is a virtual guarantee that "Tell me about XYZ" will be the first thing out of her mouth when the camera starts rolling. But this doesn't mean you shouldn't talk at all before your interview. In fact, you should talk about your IMSs in the warm-up. Just as "Don't ask me about XYZ" sets the stage for a question about XYZ, so "You know, this new asthma medication has enabled youngsters who previously were housebound to actually go out and join Little League teams" sets the stage for "I've heard that this new medication has radically improved the lives of some youngsters. Can you tell me about that?" Just be sure you remember your own story. In the Green Room before being interviewed in connection with a novel I'd written, I joked to the host of "A.M. New York," "When I was a foreign correspondent in Rome and

Berlin in the '60s, I was so poor that I couldn't afford a trench coat. All I had was an umbrella." On air, he said, "I understand you were an underpaid foreign correspondent," in hopes of eliciting the trench coat/umbrella joke. I had totally forgotten the quip and responded, "Oh, yes, I worked for a very tightfisted newspaper."

Talk Right When in the Presence of a Microphone

A microphone should be treated like a gun. Just as we are taught to treat all guns as if they are loaded, all microphones should be treated as if they are always on and broadcasting. Never say anything near a microphone that you don't want the whole world to hear. An object lesson cited by every media coach in the country is Uncle Don. It seems Uncle Don had a popular radio show for kids in the 1940s. One Friday he signed off, paused, and then said to his studio crew, "That ought to hold the little bastards for the weekend." The microphone was still switched on, the studio was still feeding audio to the air, and the little bastards— as well as many of the little bastards' parents—heard the remark. Uncle Don never returned to the air.

The truth of the matter is that the story is completely apocryphal. There was, indeed, an Uncle Don on radio in New York during the 1930s and 1940s, but if he ever referred to his listeners as little bastards, it never went out over the air. He had a long, successful career and was much loved by generations of kids and their parents. Much as I hate to lose Uncle Don as an object lesson, I still have Ronald Reagan, as you will learn in my next point.

Talk Right in a Mic Check

Before his weekly radio address one Saturday morning, President Reagan was asked for a mic check. Instead of counting from one to ten— or as rocket scientists do, from ten to one—the president decided to be funny. "Well," he said, "I've just declared war on the Soviet Union and the bombers are on their way." The remark did not go out over the air. But the reporters assembled to cover his weekly address heard it. And they printed the story. Why? Probably each reporter feared his competitors would go with the story, so each defensively wrote it to avoid being scooped. We can argue from now until the cows come home about the sanctity of the private jokes of a public person, but the fact of the matter is Reagan—who began his working life as a radio announcer—should have known better. As I have already noted, you should say *nothing* near a reporter or in proximity to a microphone that you don't want the whole wide world to hear.

You can make productive use of a mic check. Instead of counting from one to ten or down from ten to one, use the opportunity to state your name, your title, and a topic sentence to help set the agenda. If you do that, no interviewer will ever have an excuse for mispronouncing your name or for not knowing your title. And your topic sentence may well generate a question early in the interview.

Here's a sample mic check: "I'm Captain Picard, commander of the starship *Enterprise*, and I'm here today to tell you why we must defeat the Klingons." With that thought set in an interviewer's mind, it is likely that the first question will be, "Captain Picard, why do you feel we must defeat the Klingons?"

Talk Right to the Interviewer

Use the interviewer's first name—that's how the viewers know the interviewer. It's Katie, not Ms. Couric; it's Larry, not Mr. King. This is an *American* rule, by the way. Check local custom before doing it in interviews with foreign outlets like Britain's BBC, France's ORTF, or Germany's RTL. "Well, Bob . . ." is more than just a friendly gesture, by the way; it buys you some milliseconds to organize your response without appearing to be stalling. Compare that with "I'm glad you asked me that question" or the never-to-be-employed "That's a good question." Either one of these statements is likely to unleash the aggressive beast in even the most passive house pet of an inquisitor. Broadcast interviewers don't want their audience to think they are fawning fans—even if they are fawning fans. So telling them in front of those viewers that, in effect, they are giving you a "pass go, collect $200" question is likely to result in a barrage of tougher questions. Also, this may be obvious, but you should be careful not to be overly repetitive and begin every answer with "Well, Bob . . ."

When he was president, Dwight Eisenhower inaugurated the televised presidential news conference. He was counseled by his press secretary, Jim Haggerty, to buy time for an answer with a phrase like, "Let me say this about that." Good soldier that he was, Ike took the advice to heart—too much to heart. Early verbatim transcripts of his news conferences show that virtually every answer the president gave began with "Let me say this about that." Eventually, the newspapers stopped printing full verbatim transcripts. I suspect most of the material edited out was the "let me say this about that" time-buying phrase.

Leave Right

Parting may or may not be, in Shakespeare's words, "sweet sorrow," but leaving a televised interview the wrong way can give you bitter sorrow. Don't heave a sigh of relief, as if the dentist has just withdrawn his probes from your mouth and freed you from his chair. Chances are better than even that the audience will see it, and that gesture will undo much of the good you may have accomplished. Don't leap from your chair and run away. If that move is caught on camera—and Murphy's Law virtually guarantees that it will be caught on camera—the action makes you look like a fugitive. Also, it's likely that there's a microphone attached to some piece of your clothing. If it's a hardwired microphone, you're going to tear your clothing or the mic cord—or both. You should not bolt from the scene at the end of a print interview either. A reporter may well characterize your departure in her story as follows: "Obviously relieved, Mr. Y raced from the interview site even though the discussion had been conducted in his own office!"

On television, don't reach out to shake hands with your interviewer. If he extends a hand, take it, but don't initiate the gesture. Most interviewers are not expecting to have their hand shaken after an interview and may be so slow on the uptake that their body language undermines your gesture. If the interviewer offers his hand—even if he's guilty of assault with a series of deadly questions—take it and shake hands. Hemingway defined courage as "grace under pressure," so shaking hands with an interrogating bully will be perceived as courageous on your part.

Don't leave with a negative editorial comment: "Boy, you were tough on me." "Thank goodness that's over." "You never asked me about . . ."

First of all, your microphone is still on and may be transmitting. Second, that's not a good way to add information.

Just because the interview is over—even if it was a live broadcast interview—doesn't mean the information gathering is over. If something has been left out of a television interview that you think should be added, tell your interviewer in a positive way. Rather than saying, "You forgot to ask me about . . . ," try saying, "I probably should have told you . . ." The former implies the interviewer didn't do her job, whereas the latter has you taking responsibility and offering to be helpful with additional information. I have seen recorded interviews conclude with an interview subject saying something like, "You know, I probably should have talked about . . . ," and the interviewer saying, "Well, let's do a few more minutes so we can discuss that." Even live interviews afford some opportunity. I can recall a guest occasionally coming up with a good point after we had gone to commercial on "Good Morning America." If the point was of sufficient interest, sometimes David Hartman would work it in after the break, in a subsequent interview, or on another day, paraphrasing the information or using it as a basis for a question to another guest. It's not the best way to get your point across, but it's better than leaving it unspoken.

Television Interviewers: The Good, the Bad, but Never the Ugly

A few words about television interviewers: more than any other breed of journalist, television reporters serve two agendas—to get information and to look good, although not necessarily in that order. By looking good, I don't necessarily mean they want to look like a matinee idol or a soap opera star; rather, I mean looking good in the viewers' eyes and being perceived favorably. This is understandable, since television is a personality-driven business, television performers are ego-driven people, and newsrooms are not immune from the twin personality-ego viruses. The conflict between looking good and gathering information wears many faces in television. Here are a few examples:

- The reporter wants to appear tough, seasoned, and uncompromising, but the interview subject/victim is really a pitiable character. He dare not cross the line from inquisitor to bully, so he pulls back on his questioning.
- The reporter wants to appear tough and goes only for the jugular despite the fact that she knows there are mitigating facts and circumstances. She tempers anything that will make her appear compromising, even though the big compromise is with journalism's ethical standards.
- The reporter wants to appear to be friendly and charming, so he tempers his questions. During the heyday of the dot-com boom, business reporters fell over themselves doing puffball interviews with executives of start-up firms whose sole purpose for being was to make money in an initial public offering. In the cold, hard light of the economic realities of today, you would have thought that a lot of the business press were paid press agents instead of impartial journalists.
- The reporter wants to be "one of the guys." This is especially true in show business and sports interviews where the reporter wants some of a star's glitter to rub off. So instead of asking real questions, the interviewer becomes an "insider" and chats up the subject. Many interviews of movie and music stars consist of the reporter gushing all over the artist, praising her work, endorsing her projects, and then popping a mild "how do you feel about that" sort of question at her.

If you're asking yourself why you should care about reporters wanting to look good, here is the answer: you should care because if you can help the reporter achieve that goal while still serving your agenda, he will cut you a lot more slack than if you're not helping him look good.

The case of a TV or movie star is the easiest to explain. A good movie, TV, or music star makes every television interview appear to be a conversation between best friends, and most of the time by doing that the star avoids being asked embarrassing—or even substantive—questions. The stars who get beaten up by TV all the time are those who won't take a few moments to play the role of reporter's buddy. Some interviewers in the show business and sports fields can be both buddy and tough; it is a delicate balancing act, which I think Rona Barrett perfected when she was at "Good Morning America." I can recall Rona asking Gregory Peck about his son's suicide, which left the normally articulate actor momentarily wordless, and I can recall her asking Rock Hudson about a prank involving someone sending dozens of invitations to the wedding of Hudson and another prominent actor who was reputed to be gay. Hudson, stunned by the question, stopped cold, took out a cigarette, lit it, inhaled deeply, and then quietly and gently said words to the effect, "I didn't think you would ask about that." Then he added, "I thought this was a vicious and hurtful thing and while I can shrug it off, it deeply hurt a very decent human being." It was an extremely memorable moment. Had Hudson considered Rona's depth of knowledge of show business, her insider contacts, and her essential toughness, he should not have been surprised that the question came up—even from a buddy.

For those of us who are spokespersons without marquee value, a little flattery can go a long, long way. Even those on-air reporters you would think had developed immunity to flattery are suckers for a compliment or a promotional boost. For instance, consider Barbara Walters. On the first night of her brief and disastrous—and, mercifully, largely forgotten—tenure as coanchor of the "ABC Evening News," Barbara interviewed Egypt's President Anwar Sadat. Sadat was a master of the media, and he took a shot at flattery by commenting on Barbara's new million-dollar anchor contract, the very first in the history of American television news. The subsequent interview was not terribly probing. Was there a cause and effect? It's hard to say, but it didn't hurt Sadat's cause to compliment his interviewer.

It is instructional that the Sadat interview was not broadcast live but was taped and edited. ABC News elected to leave in Sadat's comment about Barbara's salary. The *New York Times* television critic pointed to its inclusion as evidence the newscast was more concerned with self-promotion than it was with news.

What do you do with the tough, hard-nosed reporter who wants to groin-kick you through five minutes of on-air time? Conventional flattery may not work. As already noted, you should avoid beginning an answer to a tough reporter's questions with, "Gee, that's a good question." That cliché is the verbal equivalent of flapping a red cape in a bull's face. The bull reporter muses, "If he thinks that's a good question, I'd better toughen up."

With this sort of reporter, you need to be more subtle. The reporter wants to appear knowledgeable and smart, and you should play to that desire. Credit the intelligence, wisdom, insight, and research behind the questions, and work that to your advantage. Rather than saying, "That's a good question," try saying, "Your question shows you have obviously done your homework and understand the issue, so no doubt you know . . ." and move on to one of your IMSs. In effect, you are saying, "You know and I know and now we'll share it with the audience so they'll know."

Understand that there are limits to this trick. Flattery is like cayenne pepper. A little goes a long way. Too much will burn you. Flatter; don't fawn.

Going "Live": Challenge or Opportunity?

As I previously indicated, the upside of a live television interview is that it is live, done in real time, and broadcast as it happens, so nothing can be edited. The downside of a live television interview is that it is live, done in real time, and broadcast as it happens, so nothing can be edited.

If you're unprepared, the lack of editing can be a daunting challenge. No one is going to fix anything for you. If your message is distorted, it will be because you distorted it, not because a producer artfully cut what you said. If you are prepared, you've got total control over everything you say, and since there's no editorial selection process, no one is going to be able to alter what you say.

Another plus/minus—depending on your level of preparation—is that live interviews tend to be much shorter than taped ones. When a correspondent or producer is taping an interview, he may revisit a question again and again, seeking the perfect soundbite or seeking to trip you up. That tactic in a live interview is a real turnoff for viewers and can make the reporter look like a bully.

There are times, though, when a bullying TV journalist can look good to viewers. That's when she's beating up on a demonstrable cad, such as the destroyer of working people's pension plans, the child abuser, or the architect of a cover-up. Mike Wallace has made a long and distinguished career out of gruff and sardonic interviews of corporate cheats, general creeps, and truly bad people. If you are a demonstrable cad, avoid both live television interviews and Mike Wallace at all costs. There is, after all, no law that says you must subject yourself to public, on-air humiliation. Following are some tips for going live.

Arrive Early

Get to the studio fifteen minutes before the time you've been given for showing up. Even if the studio is your office and a remote link has been set up for you to talk from there to the interviewer at another location, get there early. An early arrival lets you take in the geography of the studio before the interview starts, lessening the danger of distraction. Even if it's a familiar place, like your own office, the chances are something's been rearranged, and you want to notice it before your interview. Another reason to arrive early, especially for a live interview, is that you won't sit down, breathless, have a microphone pinned on, and be asked a question while you're still hyperventilating.

Warm Up

We've already dealt with the importance of the warm-up in a previous chapter. But it's worth stressing here because it's more important to plant your IMS seeds before a live interview than any other sort of interview. The reason is simple: at the end of the interview, you won't be asked that classic "anything else we should know" question. It just isn't done in live interviews. Moreover, since time in a live interview is finite and precious, you want your interviewer to have good, strong clues about what you can talk about with comfort and authority.

Be Informed

Again, as important as it is to bone up on current events for any interview, it's doubly important for a live interview. There is no way to edit out your dumbfounded surprise when the interviewer prefaces a question with, "A little while ago, before we went on the air, your agency's budget was cut by the legislature by 50 percent." I have seen numerous spokespersons—especially in the political arena—terminally embarrassed by a reporter who had information that the spokesperson should have had.

Not long ago I was media-training a number of physicists. On the way to the workshop I heard on NPR that the Nobel committee had just awarded the physics prize. "Aha," I thought. "I'll trip them up with this information." But my workshop participants had also listened to the news, and I was unable to catch them off base. Instead, we worked on using the information about the Nobel prize to explain the impact and importance of their work and how their research complemented the Nobel prizewinners' earlier work. Knowing the day's news gave their interviews a timely context.

The Preinterview

Many interview programs, and especially the live or live-to-tape programs, have staff members preinterview guests. This is done so that the on-air interviewer will have some advance idea of what a guest is going to say. You should use the preinterview to stress your IMSs to the producer or booker. Chances are she will work them into the set of questions she supplies your interviewer. On more entertainment-oriented programs like "The Late Show" or "The Tonight Show," these preinterviews are really designed to build an entertaining segment. In these cases, the writer may well suggest straight lines for you to deliver to the host or gag lines you can unleash when supplied straight lines by the host. This sort of interview is more about fun than fact, but since a lot of preparation goes into one, and since you have a very strong indication in advance of exactly where the questioning will be going, you can also figure out how to work your message points into the segment. You should always make yourself available for any preinterview. Some shows have a hard-and-fast rule that guests must submit to preinterviews or be unbooked.

When I was executive producer of "Good Morning America," we routinely unbooked guests who were uncooperative about submitting to preinterviews. The only guests exempt from preinterviews were those whose stature was extraordinarily high (president, cabinet members, heads of state). But these high-ranking officials often made available to us staff members who would stand in for their bosses in preinterviews. In general, the only guests who, as a group, routinely shunned preinterviews were top corporate executives. They not only did our staff a disservice but also did their firms a disservice because the preinterview is a useful tool for helping create the agenda for the actual interview.

Television: An Expressive Medium

More people get more information from television than from any other medium. Television is especially strong in conveying visual information or information where accompanying visuals help tell the story or illustrate the main points.

As powerful as it is for conveying information that is visual or can be supported by visuals, television is also the most collaborative of mass media. A print reporter might interview you, write a story, and then walk away from it. In television the information passes through many more hands before it reaches the end user, and the opportunity for Murphy's Law to be imposed is far greater than in other media. But television exposure is worth the challenge because it is an attention-commanding medium that customarily plays to far larger audiences than all but a handful of newspapers. Also, effective television communication skills translate well to other media and to daily communication as well.

There is, however, one branch of the television tree that requires special attention and a great deal of care if you're ever asked to appear. This is the enterprise, or investigative, program, a branch that has been growing lots of leaves lately: the hour-long investigative news shows have proliferated as the broadcast networks have sought inexpensive ways of filling their airtime without resorting to costly and risky sitcoms and drama shows. The next chapter delves into how you can master this most daunting area of television.

CHAPTER 6

DIGGING DEEP:
INVESTIGATIVE BROADCASTS

Throughout this book, I have stressed the fact that media encounters should be regarded as opportunities. I've counseled that preparation and attitude will see you through an interview and let you take control, that creating your own agenda and honing your message points will carry the day for you. Now it's time for the "yes, but . . ." exception to the rule.

"Dateline NBC," "60 Minutes," "20/20," and similar shows may present an opportunity, all right—an opportunity to hang yourself in public. These shows are unlike any other media, and they deserve separate consideration. When you're preparing to appear on one of them, you'll need to craft your singular strategy for being a successful guest on the show. To that end, the following section features background information about these shows that will help you know just what you're dealing with.

Understanding Investigative Broadcasts

When I was the executive producer of the "CBS Morning News," I would sometimes share a lunch table in the CBS Broadcast Center's basement cafeteria with Don Hewitt, the legendary creator and executive producer of "60 Minutes." At CBS News in those days one did not call the on-air result of one's work a "show" but used, instead, the term "broadcast," as in, "That was a fine broadcast this morning."

Presumably, a "show" had the stink of entertainment about it, the unsavory aroma of show business, perhaps even a whiff of sensationalism. "Broadcast" was a more dignified term befitting our journalistic product. Since I had been reared in the scrappy, unpretentious precincts of ABC, I repeatedly made the mistake of referring to the "Morning News" as a "show." What began as a slip of the tongue eventually became an exercise in rebellion; I delighted in the "punch to the solar plexus" wince the "s" word elicited from CBS News old-timers, so I used it a lot.

The only other person at CBS News who called what he produced a "show" was Don Hewitt. He wasn't being rebellious—he was being accurate. I've heard Hewitt say that "60 Minutes" is a prime-time show about the adventures of (at that time) four men who, like the iconic heroes of old Westerns, rode into town and righted wrongs. Instead of U.S. marshals or Texas Rangers, these four cowboys happened to be newsmen. Hewitt's on-screen "magnificent four" back then were Morley Safer, Ed Bradley, Harry Reasoner, and Mike Wallace.

I'm telling you all of this so you'll understand that "60 Minutes" and its many imitators, like "20/20," "Dateline NBC," and "60 Minutes II," are not designed to offer fair, impartial renderings of fact. Rather, they are information-based entertainment vehicles, designed to excite an emotional response from viewers. The fact that they do it better than many drama shows is a testament to the skill of their correspondents and producers, who, after all, must work essentially with words spoken by others rather than words crafted by writers. Broadcasting's investigative cowboys load their six-shooters with interview subjects' words—and often shoot the interview subject right between the eyes with those words. If you end up on one of these shows, you must be sure not to give the gunslingers any ammunition they can use against you.

So what should you do when the producer for one of these investigative shows calls for an interview? Do you blow them off? Do you embrace the opportunity? Do you send someone else into the jaws of hell? Well, you should decide what to do depending on whether you are being cast as a good guy or a bad guy.

Are You a Good Guy or a Bad Guy?

It is a rule of the theater, movies, and television that you cannot have drama without conflict. You cannot have conflict without at least two contending sides. On one side of the conflict is the hero. On the other side of the conflict is the villain. Good guys versus bad guys. So it is on the reality-based dramas presented by the investigative shows. When that friendly producer from one of them phones you to talk about a story, the first question to ask yourself is, "Am I a good guy or a bad guy?"

The following persons are almost always good guys:

- environmentalists, unless they commit acts of sabotage, desecration, or physical violence
- firefighters, unless they are arsonists
- poor people, unless they are criminals
- one-person law firms whose one lawyer dresses in Wal-Mart suits

The following persons are almost always bad guys:

- polluters, or anyone who can be construed as a polluter
- rich people, unless they got rich by being actors, singers, comedians, or novelists
- partners in large law firms who wear $2,500 suits

Despite these lists, there are no pat answers as to who is a bad guy and who is a good guy. "60 Minutes," in particular, revels in the unpredictable and will frequently lionize those whom conventional wisdom has branded the bad guys and skewer those whom conventional wisdom has adorned with the good guy mantle. Just because you've always gotten praise from the rest of the press, there's no reason to assume one of these shows has joined the bandwagon. In fact, there's a good chance the show may be trying to flatten the bandwagon's tires.

On the air, "60 Minutes" usually gives us subtle visual clues about who is a bad guy and who is a good guy. In fact, you can tell one from the other with the volume off! Everyone—save the show's aging talent—is shot in extreme close-up. But bad guys tend to be shot from closer up and from a slightly lower angle. The unflattering "up the nostrils" shot is customarily reserved for the villains. The slightly wider framing, shot from eye level or slightly above, is reserved for the good guys. The other nonfiction drama shows don't go in for this visual gimmick, although they do like it if the bad guy sweats on camera. Another visual clue is B-roll of the correspondent strolling along, talking to an interview subject. Typically, the stroll is reserved for the good guy because it visually tells the audience the correspondent is on the side of—or alongside—the interview subject.

Obviously, it's too late to prepare your defensive strategy if you learn you're the bad guy after the microphone is pinned on and the camera starts shooting up your nostrils. So you must determine in advance whether you're going to be standing shoulder to shoulder with the news lawman or facing him across the O.K. Corral. A little later on in this chapter, I'll give you some tips for determining on which side an investigative show has cast you.

What's a Good Guy to Do?

This one is simple. If you're confident that you are a good guy, proceed with the investigative show interview exactly as you would with any other television interview. Prepare your IMSs, anticipate questions, practice your answers, and you should emerge not merely unscathed but enshrined.

What's a Bad Guy to Do?

If you find that Wyatt Earp and his brothers, along with their pal Doc Holliday, are oiling their six-shooters and practicing their quick draw for a confrontation with you, what's your move? Do you saddle up and ride out of town or do you stand up to them? Let me give you two case histories that are valid object lessons when dealing with investigative shows. The main point in each lesson is to always be fully aware of what the true purpose of the show will be.

Case History 1: Blocking the Story

A foreign-owned automobile company that assembled some of its cars in the United States brought me in to prepare some spokespersons for interviews on a network investigative newsmagazine show. A confidentiality agreement prevents me from revealing the company name and even its home base nation, so let's call them Quickcar Motors of Carland.

"What's the story?" I asked.

"Oh," said the Quickcar Motors domestic publicity chief, "they're going to do a story about how our local plant uses the same production techniques we use in Carland and how that's revolutionizing assembly-line work in the U.S."

Resisting the urge to sell him oceanfront property in Nebraska and a bridge between Manhattan and Brooklyn, I asked, "Have you ever seen that show do an industrial story? What are they really after? What controversies are brewing in your assembly plant?"

After several minutes of insisting that a network producer wouldn't lie to him and that the Carland production techniques were a great story, he dug deep and admitted that some workers had been expressing grievances about perceived on-the-job racial and gender discrimination. He hastened to tell me the grievances were completely unwarranted.

"Warranted or unwarranted, that's the story they are after," I said, "not how foreign production techniques are working in the U.S. The discrimination charge is an investigative story—conflict, good guys, bad guys. Building cars the way they do in Carland has no conflict and no real bad guys."

"But there's no merit to the grievances," the publicity man protested.

It didn't matter, I told him. This particular company had always enjoyed glowing reviews for its products, and this was just the sort of big, brightly lit window the investigative reporters enjoy shattering with a well-aimed brick.

My client could have been blindsided with the discrimination accusations had he submitted to the interview without identifying the true purpose of the story, no matter how unwarranted the accusations may have been. On camera, the spokesperson might well have sputtered and stammered defensively, ill equipped to cite exculpatory statistics. It would have been "guilt by appearance."

I urged my client to take the calculated risk of not letting the show's camera videotape in the plant. I figured that the story was so heavily dependent on production-line images, it could not be told without in-plant footage. Also, I suggested making available only lower-level assembly-line engineering types for interviews—people who could not be asked about personnel issues. I was right; the show dropped the story. You, too, without the benefit of my experience in the media, may be able to block a story by preventing it from being shot, so long as you understand what the real scoop is and what it will take in terms of footage for the broadcast to achieve its goal.

That said, the danger in my approach was that the show might have stationed one of its reporters in front of the plant saying something like, "They wouldn't let us in," using that fact as an indication of "guilt." That stunt would have been pretty good biased journalism but very lame television. It works on the local news where the average story is less than two minutes long, but the investigative magazine shows are, after all, built around point-counterpoint confrontations running ten minutes or so. Point-point is poor drama and cannot be stretched to ten minutes.

Case History 2: Emerging from the O.K. Corral Unscathed

Not everyone can shut out the investigative shows. Public agencies, for example, usually can't deny access even to the most predatory journalists, so their spokespersons have to do the best they can to deny the reporters anything to chew on.

A few years ago I prepared a government agency spokesman for an investigative segment on one of the network newsmagazine shows. He knew he was going to be the bad guy. The segment was about a controversial government-sponsored endeavor, and because this one had high visibility, the show's producer made no pretense about the subject of the report when calling to book my client.

I asked the spokesman's public relations person to tell the show that the agency was going to videotape the interview. The producer couldn't very well say no, since he was going to have two cameras in the conference room where the interview was to take place. You should definitely use videotape for archiving this type of show and not audiotape, which is adequate for most interviews. Videotape will keep the correspondent exceptionally honest when it comes time to edit his story.

Use assertive language to discuss your videotaping of the interview. An example of this would be, "We're going to tape the interview for internal purposes; we assume that presents no problem to you?" Not, "Would it be all right if we tape the interview, too?" Assert—don't request. And be sure that your camera is aimed not at the spokesperson but at the correspondent asking the questions. More on taping a potentially hostile interview a little later.

The tape made by my client of his investigative interview was an education in and of itself. In his forty-minute interview, the correspondent used every trick enumerated in "The Interviewer's Top Seven Dirty Tricks" in Chapter 4. In fact, he used most of them three and four times. He also asked the same questions three, four, and five times, hoping that my client would get so bored with his answers, he would vary them and hang himself.

But the spokesperson had already been asked all those questions. Repeatedly. First by me and then by his public relations department. Many hours of intensive mock hostile interviewing enabled him to answer the tough questions and remain totally in control. Moreover, his preparation allowed him to remain so calm and unemotional that he gave the program nothing to use: no embarrassing statements, no nervous stammering, no flashes of anger. In fact, the program didn't use one second of the interview they taped with him because my client refused to play his assigned role: the bad guy. So the show had to go out and find another spokesperson to skewer.

You, too, through diligent practice and a calm demeanor can succeed in maintaining your cool and not appearing to be the bad guy the program may wish to make you into.

Girding for Battle

Whether you're the good guy or bad guy being interviewed for an investigative broadcast, there are seven specific rules of engagement you must follow to make sure you give the most effective interview possible:

1. Determine what role you've been assigned.
2. Determine what the "other side" will say.
3. Write out the interviewer's questions.
4. Craft your rebuttal/message points.
5. Rehearse the interview.
6. Record the interview.
7. Seize the initiative.

Rule 1: Determine What Role You've Been Assigned

In the two case histories I cited, one client did not know if he was the good guy or the bad guy, and the other was sure he was the bad guy. Ask yourself the following questions to determine if you've been cast as the villain:

- **Were you or was your organization a source in the researching of the story?** These shows cost a lot to produce, so they don't just go out and shoot a story. If they try to book you for an interview without having spoken to you at length beforehand, chances are they want to hear what you have to say only when the camera is rolling. In other words, their minds are already made up. If you answered "No" to this question, chances are you're the bad guy.
- **Does the producer's description of the show's story sound like the sort of stories that show normally airs?** If you answered "No," then you're probably being misled about the real story the show's doing. As a general rule, only bad guys are misled.
- **In the preinterview, did the producer try to get you to comment off the record or were there echoes of the "other side's" ideas in her questions or attitude?** If you answered "Yes," prepare for a hostile interview.

Rule 2: Determine What the "Other Side" Will Say

Try to learn who your opponents are. Ask the producer or reporter who calls to book you if he will send you (by fax or E-mail) a list of everyone else who will be interviewed for the story as well as everyone he's spoken to in researching the story. If you ask for this list to be given to you verbally, chances are it will be less complete than if you ask for it in writing. Still, the list he sends you may omit key opponents. If several obvious adversaries are not on the list, make your own list. Also, if a list is refused, prepare your own list of those you know to be hostile to your position.

Here's an offensive tip: whether or not you get a list, recommend—in writing—additional people for the producer to talk with. These should be individuals unaffiliated with your enterprise who agree with your point of view. Your recommendations may be ignored, but if they are not, you've given the show some leads that will buttress your side.

Using either the producer's list or your own—preferably both—prepare a list of the points you anticipate your opponents will make. Be specific; your opponents will be specific, and the interviewer will craft his questions from those specifics. Put yourself into your opponent's head. Ask yourself what she will have told the producer or reporter off camera to entice him to do this story. Remember, the more sensational the charge, the more attractive it is to the producer, so don't hold back, even if her assertions are preposterous! Your list is best prepared on a computer so you can cut and paste and insert your rebuttal material.

Rule 3: Write Out the Interviewer's Questions

Below each of your opponent's points, write a tough, hostile question based on that point. Don't be diplomatic or shy. Make the questions pointed, direct, and stinging. If you're prepared for the tough questions, you can handle the easy ones. If you're only prepared for the easy questions, the tough ones will throw you.

Rule 4: Craft Your Rebuttal/Message Points

After you've written out all the interviewer's possible points, the next step is to craft a counterargument for each point. Insert the rebuttal point into your document right after the tough question. It is not enough to merely defend yourself in these situations because you don't want to appear to be fighting a rearguard action. Your points should be positive expressions of your side of the argument.

Rule 5: Rehearse the Interview

Unless you have an abnormal masochistic streak, you cannot interview yourself with adequate intensity and hostility to prepare for an interview by a broadcast investigative reporter. Get someone to throw your tough questions at you in a challenging manner. If your questioner is a subordinate, assure him you won't hold his demeanor against him at review time.

Have your interrogator mimic an investigative reporter, asking the same question repeatedly and in a skeptical voice; insist he show you no mercy. Have your colleague read the interviewer's "dirty tricks" enumerated in Chapter 4 before he grills you. Videotape the session so you can watch it later and analyze the quality of your responses. Do it over and over again until you can ignore the attitude of the questions and deal only with their substance.

Become comfortable building bridges from tough questions to your rebuttal points. Remember the lesson of Chapter 4: it's often easier to bridge from a tough, hostile question to an IMS than it is to navigate from a friendly but off-the-point query. Do not attempt to memorize word for word your rebuttal points; you don't want to sound like a zombie repeating preprogrammed answers. On the other hand, you should be so familiar with your material that you can take advantage of any opportunity to score your rebuttal points.

Review the tape of your practice interview and critique yourself mercilessly. Then repeat the exercise. See how many of your rebuttal points you are able to work into the interview. Critique each interview. Repeat the exercise again and again. Remember that any of these investigative shows may interview you for—well, sixty minutes. They may have at you for an hour or more until you hang yourself with an incriminating ten-second soundbite. It's better to have a colleague beat you up with these questions in the privacy of your own office than to have Mike Wallace do it with the whole world watching. Steve Kroft, another "60 Minutes" reporter, once said, "We always know the answers to the questions before we ask them." It's likely that Kroft and his colleagues don't really know what the answers will be before the questions are posed, though they likely know what they want the answers to be. If you don't play along and give the anticipated answer, the correspondent will probably keep asking the question in different words, hoping you'll eventually answer it the way he has written it down.

Rule 6: Record the Interview

Record the actual interview with a video camera. Tell the producer and interviewer you are recording the session; it does you less good to have a spycam somewhere in your office than it does to let them know they are being archived just as they are archiving you. Be aware that it's illegal in some states to clandestinely record another person, and it's of dubious morality even where it's legal. Taping the interview prevents the worst sins of creative editing: putting answer B to question A and pulling only incriminating phrases from answers.

When you record the interview, point your video camera at the interviewer, not at yourself. This helps keep theatrical reactions to your answers—raised eyebrows, dubious nods, and so on—to a minimum.

Rule 7: Seize the Initiative

If you think your interview has gone badly and you feel you've suffered a disaster at the hands of an investigative reporter, you should consider taking the initiative and getting out in front of the story. These newsmagazine broadcasts can't move as fast as a daily news show or a newspaper, so mobilize all of your organization's publicity apparatuses to get the story out to the public before it airs. Tell the story from your point of view and tell it with as much fanfare as you can.

The Investigative Interview

As for the investigative interview itself, all the rules of interviews—and all the rules for television interviews specifically—apply. Read the papers and listen to newscasts or check online news sources immediately before your interview. You don't want to be caught flat-footed, not knowing late-breaking developments.

- **Arrive early.** Even if the interview is in your own office, be there while the crews are setting up; that way you won't be distracted by the equipment and personnel new to the room or by the inevitable rearrangement that occurs every time a TV crew sets up in a location.
- **Eat something.** You don't want your blood sugar level plummeting during an interview. Avoid alcohol, dairy products, and caffeine— alcohol does not calm you, but lulls you; milk, cream, and other dairy products produce phlegm, which can make your voice very unattractive; and the caffeine can make you hyperactive.
- **Greet and chat with the producer and correspondent.** Under normal circumstances it is tougher for a reporter to beat up on someone she feels she knows than to beat up on someone she doesn't know, but investigative reporters are generally immune to this sentiment. Nevertheless, chatting in advance doesn't do any harm so long as you don't get lulled into a false sense of security by the reporter's or producer's friendly attitude. If you're the bad guy, the assault is coming, no matter how friendly the person is when exchanging preinterview small talk.
- **Expect the worst.** Unless you are the good guy, you're going to be subjected to every one of the interviewer's "dirty tricks" (see Chapter 4) in your interview, and you're going to be subjected to them repeatedly. The pregnant pause, the misrepresentation of your answers, the incredulous repetition of your words, the out-of-left-field hypotheticals, and the accusatory tone—all of these will come at you time and again.

  Don't let these techniques shake you. The reason the reporter will continue to hammer away with these tricks is simply this: she wants to shake your composure and get you to change your stand, and she wants you to appear defensive. Stick to your answers, don't change them for the sake of change, don't waver from your rebuttal points, don't compromise, and don't let the interviewer pressure you into retreating. Above all, remain calm, composed, unshakable, and positive—and, in spite of the repeated assaults with deadly questions, stay friendly. The reporter knows that if she gets too hostile with someone who remains reasonable and friendly, she's the one who will lose the audience's sympathy. A final reminder on the pause: in this type of interview, do not take advantage of a reporter's pause in the questioning. Normally, when a reporter stops, she is busy searching her papers for her next question and it's a good time for you to insert a message. In an investigative or hostile interview, the pause is a trick to get you to expand on an answer you've already given.

Postinterview

When the interview is over—finally!—don't beat a hasty retreat. Instead, stick around while the crew and interviewer pack up, and act as if there are no hard feelings—even if there are. Feel free to suggest additional rebuttal points and other people the interviewer can speak to and other research material she might consult. Keep your discussion on point and positive and don't volunteer anything negative because it could wind up in her completed story, with or without attribution to you.

If there are valid rebuttal points you haven't made, send them (by fax, E-mail, or mail) to the correspondent with copies to her producer and executive producer. At the very least, they are ethically bound to consider these points for inclusion in the finished piece, and you will be on record as having proffered them.

After the interview, take the time to analyze your tape of the session. A careful analysis of how you answered will benefit your future interviews. Also, if others who share your point of view are yet to be interviewed, you can give them a heads-up about the reporter's specific questions and her techniques.

Beaten Up and Bloodied, but Not Defeated

If the story airs and seriously misrepresents you or your organization, don't sit quietly by. Complain to everyone and anyone who will listen. Show your tape of the interview to TV critics, journalism professors, and local affiliates of the network that misrepresented you. Send copies of your tape of the interview and a tape of the actual report as broadcast to all of these people and to the president of the offending news division and to her network boss as well. One word of warning, however: do this only if the misrepresentation is serious, not simply because you've got a bruised ego or because you misspoke on camera.

For example, I can recall a complaint lodged with the president of ABC Television about a segment I produced concerning ARAMCO, the Arab-American Oil Company. An ARAMCO official claimed we'd misrepresented him when we showed him saying that, despite the fact that ARAMCO was a publicly traded American company, he owed his first loyalty to "his majesty the king" of Saudi Arabia. When we had filmed the interview, we'd been stunned by this answer, and the correspondent, David Schoumacher, asked him the question again. And again. The executive had three chances to give a different answer, but he repeated the "his majesty the king" answer each time.

After the complaint, the president of the network came to our edit suite and screened the entire interview. I stood by outside the room, nervously awaiting his judgment and imagining my career going down the drain. When he emerged, the network president said words to this effect: "I can see why he's upset, but he not only said it, he said it three times. He should have thought about how it would sound before he opened his mouth, not after we aired it." That's good advice. When you are practicing, think of how your answers will sound in the context of the story the reporter is preparing. You may want to hone them to an even sharper edge before you submit to the interview.

The experience of appearing on an investigative television news program, while not very common, can be extremely intimidating should you find yourself called to the task. Regardless, the same tips and techniques needed to effectively navigate these interviews will help you conduct successful interviews at all levels. Two other somewhat rare, but equally intimidating, interviewing experiences are the ambush interview and the shoutfest. Both are covered in the next chapter.

CHAPTER 7

BUSHWHACKED:
HOW TO SURVIVE AN AMBUSH INTERVIEW AND WIN A SHOUTFEST

Two of television's biggest interview challenges are the ambush interview and the shoutfest. While they are very different experiences, they do share two characteristics: neither is pleasant and neither is particularly conducive to expressing your agenda. In an ambush interview, the chances are good you'll be caught totally unawares and have no agenda prepared. In a shoutfest, you'll go into the studio with an agenda, but to be heard over the competing roars of the other guests is the challenge. However, you can survive an ambush and you can get your points into even the windiest of shoutfests by putting into practice the following advice.

Ambush Interviews

The ambush interview has been around a long time. Reporters used ambushes before there was television news or even television. On television, ambush interviews rarely shed much light, but they often generate a lot of heat. And heat translates to one of the demands of our visual medium: good theater.

An ambush consists of a journalist accosting an unsuspecting—and often unwilling—interview subject in an unexpected location and throwing a succession of questions at him. This can happen both in print and on TV.

If you don't answer a print reporter's ambush questions, she is likely to write, "Mr. Richards refused comment" or "Confronted with questions outside his office, Mr. Richards declined to comment for this article." That's a lot less damaging to Mr. Richards than the television depiction of that same refusal to talk, especially if that refusal is demonstrated by a hasty retreat. What could be better theater than the video image of a portly corporate executive in a gray suit running down a street with a reporter in hot pursuit shouting questions after him? The image is a visual nolo contendere plea to any charge the reporter cares to make.

Geraldo Rivera, network newsmagazine shows, and most local station investigative reporters love the ambush. Today, in fact, bushwhacking almost anyone passes for investigative journalism at a distressing number of local television stations across the country.

Typically, the unsuspecting and unprepared bushwhackee is accosted in the open—so he can run away and be taped doing it—say, between his office building and his car or in front of the Chuck E. Cheese's restaurant after his kid's birthday party. It's the contemporary equivalent of a Western gunslinger's quick drawing on someone between the swinging doors of the saloon and the hitching post where his horse is tethered.

The camera is rolling and the microphone is pointed like a six-shooter at the subject's throat. There are no niceties, no "Good afternoon, sir, may we ask you a few questions?" There is just the challenging first question, usually shouted at top volume, and, if the bushwhackee doesn't answer instantly, several more rapid-fire questions, often without time in between for an answer even if the victim wants to talk.

If you find yourself in this situation, don't run away! Instead, stand your ground and talk to the reporter. This isn't the time to have an open and friendly conversation with the reporter because it's likely you will be positioned as the bad guy, and it's equally likely you're not prepared to discuss any intentional message statements. That said, there are some things you *should* say to the reporter, but before getting into what you should say, first let me tell you what *not* to say. Don't say what the following black-belt bushwhacker did when the tables were turned and he was ambushed in front of his office.

The perpetrator of this ambush was Steve Wilson, a very aggressive investigative reporter then working on a syndicated daily newsmagazine show. And Steve's victim was none other than a network correspondent whose own ambush interviews used to give Geraldo Rivera a run for his money as the *bushwhacker di tutti bushwhacki*. The supreme irony here is that Steve's ambush of the correspondent was a direct result of a failed ambush by the correspondent.

Sometime earlier, Steve's target had been doing a story about a store-front physician in Los Angeles who, the program contended, was faking injury reports in an auto insurance scam. The correspondent accosted his prey in the parking lot of the clinic. For some reason, the man had a camera hanging from a strap around his neck. Instead of answering questions, he did what every ambusher hopes his target will do—he ran away. But every so often, he stopped fleeing, turned around, and took photographs of the pursuing correspondent and his crew. It turned out the correspondent and crew had the wrong man; the photographing prey was not the doctor. Naturally, the sequence wasn't used in the story about the doctor. But when the real doctor sued the network for libel, all the film taken for the report was introduced into evidence in court.

At the time, I was executive producer of "Entertainment Tonight," and our enterprising reporter covering the story, Scott Osborne, asked the judge whether or not the outtakes—as evidence—weren't public record. The judge agreed and turned over the outtakes to Osborne. We ran a story about the case and featured the correspondent chasing the wrong man.

A little while later, Steve Wilson, following up on that story, ambushed the correspondent as he emerged from his office building. When Wilson popped a tough question at him, the correspondent pulled Wilson's microphone very close and, leaning into it, very clearly and deliberately enunciated, "[Expletive] you. You got that?" And just in case Wilson hadn't gotten it, the correspondent repeated it, "[Expletive] you."

Wilson was speechless. The correspondent walked away, no doubt confident he had given Wilson nothing that could be aired. Like President Reagan with his mic check attempt at humor, the correspondent should have known better. Not only did Wilson's show air a report on the encounter (with the expletive bleeped but clearly discernible to anyone who had gotten beyond the fourth grade), but they made a copy of the tape available to "Entertainment Tonight," and we ran it, too.

Now you're probably asking, "If I don't take flight and if I don't unleash my expletive vocabulary, what do I do if I'm ambushed by a TV reporter?" There are two hard-and-fast rules for surviving an ambush attack: (1) don't run away: you will appear to be—and, in fact, you will be—a fugitive from the newsman and the public and (2) don't give an ambusher an interview.

First and foremost, you need to get out of the situation in the least hostile and least dramatic manner possible. To do so, you should calmly say, "I'd love to help you with your story, but I can't do it right now because . . ." Select an appropriate excuse from the inventory that follows; use whichever one is true:

- "I've got a meeting I must attend immediately, and I wouldn't want to give this subject short shrift. So call my office and arrange a proper sit-down interview."
- "I'm not totally current with the subject, and I think it would be a disservice to you and your viewers if I gave uninformed comments. So call my office and arrange a proper sit-down interview."
- "Company policy prohibits talking about a case in litigation." (This is obviously to be used only in connection with a matter that is in litigation.)
- "The judge has imposed a gag order, and I can't in good conscience violate that order. What you're asking me to do is break the law." (This is to be used only in connection with a matter that is in litigation where a judge has, indeed, issued a gag order.)

Notice in the first two instances you have stated a desire to help the reporter and have invited him to call you for an appointment. His response will likely be more shouted questions or even threats such as, "Well, we're going to have to go without your side of the story." Remain calm and unmoved and don't give him a single soundbite beyond saying, "I'm sorry you feel the need to go with incomplete information, but I've explained that I'm willing to talk to you at a later time." He will probably keep sticking the microphone in your face in hopes of vexing you into an outburst or a flight, but resist the urge to shout or flee; it's unlikely he'll ever use on the air your calm invitation to him to a sit-down interview because it would raise the question in the viewer's mind of why he didn't just take you up on that invitation.

At this point, you should understand that the ambush interview on television is a theatrical, not a journalistic, tactic, and in the event that you find yourself in this situation, you should play the role of the sober, reasoned, cooperative-albeit-unavailable statesman. If you do that, you've taken all the drama from this particular aspect of the reporter's story, and it's not worth showing. For example, had the correspondent said to Steve Wilson, "I'm sorry, Steve, but I'm late for an interview of my own and I have to leave now, but I'll be happy to talk with you at a later time and date," "Entertainment Tonight" would never have run the clip. In fact, the correspondent had an even better calm and rational way out of the ambush. Wilson's story did involve a legal case, so company policy against commenting on a case in litigation would have been a completely legitimate excuse for not speaking with him.

If you saw the recent Michael Moore documentary *Bowling for Columbine*, you can take as an object lesson Moore's ambush of Dick Clark. In the film, Moore approaches Clark, who is sitting in the backseat of a minivan with the sliding door wide open. The minivan's motor is running, Clark is talking to the driver, and it is obvious that he is in a rush to get somewhere.

Without explaining what the interview is about, Moore begins peppering Clark with questions. Moore is trying to pin Clark down because the very young son of a welfare-to-work employee at a Clark-owned restaurant in Michigan found a gun in his uncle's home, took it to school, and killed a classmate. Moore's contention is pretty far-fetched. He feels that the welfare-to-work program deprived the child of adequate parental supervision and that Clark shares responsibility for the tragedy because he—albeit not he personally—provided the mother with her job. As the questioning begins, Clark is unaware of the subject and so answers the first couple of questions, although it is clear from his tone and attitude that this is a major inconvenience and he is in a desperate rush to get somewhere.

Quickly, Clark realizes that this is a hostile ambush for which he is totally unprepared, and he snaps to the driver of the van, "Let's get going," and vigorously slides the door shut. Watching the movie, I was shocked at Moore's wild and less-than-responsible effort to connect Dick Clark with the school shooting, but others I spoke with after seeing the film said they thought Moore had done a good job of "getting" Clark.

Well, in point of fact, Clark got himself. The tie between Clark and the shooting was so tenuous that it bordered on the ludicrous to try to make the connection. However, by reacting emotionally, Clark gave Moore all the drama the filmmaker needed.

It is more than likely that the encounter would not have made it into the completed film had Clark said, "I'm sorry, Michael. But as you can see, we're on our way to a meeting and we're running late. I'd be happy to talk to you sometime, but you have to understand that I'm really very busy right now. Why don't you call my office and set something up. Again, sorry, but we've got to go; we can't keep these people waiting." Then Clark could have gently slid the door closed and had his driver pull away. That would have given Moore nothing terribly dramatic or comedic.

In that scenario, when Moore called the office, Clark's staff could have learned the purpose of the interview and Clark could have made an informed decision about whether or not he wanted to participate. Had he not participated, the worst Moore could have done was stand outside Clark's Burbank office building or Michigan restaurant and announce to the camera, "Dick Clark refused to talk to us."

Dick Clark is about as accomplished an interview subject as there is on the planet, so if he can be tricked into giving Michael Moore the bit of good theater Moore was looking for, what chance do the rest of us mere mortals have? Probably a better chance, in fact. Most interviews with Dick Clark are about his large number of successful entertainment projects, so he's accustomed to giving interviewers his time because it is usually to his benefit to do so. It's likely he is habitually less on his guard against a hostile interview—especially one from so far off in left field—than you or I would be.

The bottom line is, if a camera appears out of nowhere and it's accompanied by an aggressive reporter shouting questions, you're being ambushed. You cannot win one of these encounters because you won't be prepared, so you need to excuse yourself and gracefully avoid the encounter by inviting the reporter to meet with you in a more formal setting. Next to an ambush, a televised shoutfest is a picnic, an opportunity for you to shoehorn in some of your messages despite some daunting challenges.

How to Win a Shoutfest

There is a trend in television news interview programs that is distressing for those who actually want to glean some information from them: they are increasingly becoming shoutfests with adherents thinking they "win" by drowning out opponents. Audiences must be responding to this heat-over-light approach because the ranks of these unpleasant exercises in sound and fury are multiplying, while the serious journalistic efforts like "Nightline" and "The NewsHour with Jim Lehrer" remain exceptions rather than the rule. In general, shoutfests deal with political and social matters. If you are the spokesperson for a political, a social, or even an economic issue that could spark controversy, you are likely to be invited on such a program. If you are the spokesperson for a new product or service or scientific breakthrough, you are unlikely to find yourself subjected to one of these raucous encounters.

The first rule of thumb if you're scheduled to appear on a shoutfest-style program is to watch the program itself so you can identify the style and agenda of the interviewer or host. Most of the hosts on these shows have an ideological agenda, and it's best to know if he's on the side of your angels or your devils. Watching will also give you insights into how far he'll let the talk-over go before intervening and letting individuals have their say.

Preparation is, as always, the key to winning a shoutfest, and in a shoutfest you need to sloganeer. Prepare your slogans by reducing your IMSs to their barest essentials, or the equivalent to verbal headlines. When you're on the air, simply shout them unabashedly into the fray whenever you can, usually when an opponent takes a breath. Even the most long-winded must draw as well as expel air.

In a shoutfest, all rules of etiquette are thrown out the window. You don't need to be responding to a question and there need be no context to your IMSs; you need only the space to ram them in. All that viewers are hearing is babble anyway, so if you can launch an IMS in the clear, the audience is going to assume it had a context. It's possible your IMS will lead the moderator to follow up with a direct question or, at least, steer the discussion into consideration of what you want to talk about. In addition, it's important in the shoutfest not to get drawn too deeply into your opponent's tirade, lest you wind up just shouting responses no one is going to hear anyway. And you really don't want to address his points or, at least, you don't want to answer them in any detail, because if you do, you're serving his agenda and his points will be heard twice, and that's what the viewers will be more likely to remember.

While it makes no conversational sense at all to participate in a discussion about a particular topic in this way, just watch the shows: what does make sense on a shoutfest? These shows feature three, four, or five people trying to outyell each other, all speaking at the same time—if speaking isn't too mild a word for it—with complex issues reduced to slogans. If you can deliver the few seconds of light amid the many minutes of heat, you've gone a long way toward winning.

Neither an ambush nor a shoutfest is the ideal venue for expressing your intentional message statements. In the first, you probably will be accosted without any IMSs at hand. You may be able to dredge some up from memory, but it's just not worth the effort to do it; you're better off excusing yourself from the encounter and inviting the reporter to speak with you when you will have had time to prepare for her onslaught. In the latter, you find yourself in a competition that is more theatrical than journalistic. The shoutfest places a greater value on the entertainment aspects of passionate yelling and mindless invective than it does on the intellectual content of your statements. Far more civil— and far more conducive to calm, rational, and even *thorough* expressions of ideas—are print and online interviews. And those are the media we'll deal with in our next chapter.

CHAPTER 8

TAKING NOTES:
PRINT AND ONLINE
INTERVIEWS

The oldest of the mass media and the youngest share more similarities than differences. Stories in print publications and Internet news outlets are more often the work of a single reporter than of
a team (common in broadcasting). Moreover, both generally have more
space than broadcast media has time to devote to a story, and both
are great venues for analytical journalism and think pieces. Since print
has been around longer and since you are more likely to encounter print
interviews than online interviews, let's deal with that venerable medium
first.

Print Interviews

Print was the first mass medium and to this day is generally the most
thorough of all the various forms of media. Movable type, perfected by
Johannes Gutenberg in the fifteenth century, enabled printers to report
the news right after it happened. With the spread of literacy, newspaper readership exploded, reaching impressive heights in America during the early to mid-twentieth century. In those times, competition for
readers and for advertising dollars was, for the most part, among the
print outlets, not between them and other media. In cities such as New
York, there were more than a dozen daily English-language newspapers
as well as dailies printed in Chinese, Greek, Italian, Russian, and Yid-
dish. Weekly community and ethnic newspapers brought the total num-

ber of newsy journals in that city alone to more than one hundred! Even back in 1961, when I graduated from Columbia University's School of Journalism, there remained four citywide mass-circulation morning daily newspapers and three afternoon dailies. Today, only three of those seven survive, which is two more daily newspapers than most American cities have.

While the commodity of the broadcast media is time, the equivalent commodity in print journalism is space. On a big news day a paper can add space by simply adding pages. It can get bigger or smaller as dictated both by the space needs of the day's news and by the requirements of display and classified advertising. An hour of broadcast time—or any time—is fixed by the speed of the earth's rotation. It is an absolute: sixty minutes. An hour cannot be expanded to sixty-two minutes to accommodate a big story. And, in fact, that broadcast hour is really closer to forty-four minutes, once you subtract the time for commercials. If you're thinking that's skimpy, consider that the ratio of editorial content to advertising is four-to-one in broadcasting but more like one-to-one in print. In fact, some newspapers print more advertising than news, especially in their Sunday editions. The corollary to the reread factor, which enables you to go back in a newspaper or magazine and reread a sentence or paragraph, is the disregard factor. You can toss out those advertising supplements on Sunday, skip by the display ads, and just concentrate on the news story that runs alongside. The only ways to do that in a linear medium like television is to use the commercial breaks to go to the refrigerator or the bathroom or to buy and use a device like the TiVo, which can record the news and be programmed to skip the commercials when playing back. But, for most TV viewers and for all radio listeners, the broadcast media are not random-access information sources, the way publications are.

Despite the impressive content-to-advertising ratio in broadcasting, on a routine basis the print media allot far more space to news than broadcast allots the equivalent time. When I worked on newspapers, all the space devoted to material other than advertising and regular features like stock tables and comic strips was called, rather inelegantly, the news hole. In the middle of the twentieth century, when there were so many newspapers looking for material to fill their news holes, legions of print reporters worked the streets and phones to develop stories. While the ranks of publications, especially dailies, have thinned and the legions of print reporters have become squads, print remains the medium where your message is likely to get its most thorough examination. So it's important to consider how you can best communicate to readers through the remaining inky wretches who practice the ancient craft of print journalism.

The Grammatical Imperative

Back in the 1960s when I was a reporter for the now-defunct *New York World-Telegram and Sun*, the city's mayor was an affable career politician named Robert F. Wagner Jr. Mayor Wagner came by his skills naturally; his father had been a U.S. senator and a major player in the creation of Franklin D. Roosevelt's New Deal. Mayor Wagner served three four-year terms, leading the city through a variety of crises with effective solutions but little flair. While the mayor was a liberal Democrat, he shared one trait with the current conservative Republican president, George W. Bush: he routinely butchered English syntax when he spoke off-the-cuff. I cannot recall the mayor making up new words like *explanify*, but like the president, he was capable of torturing grammar until it screamed for mercy.

Just as routinely as Mayor Wagner tore sentences apart, reporters put them back together for him—and for their readers. Back then, if you read an account of the same mayoral press conference in all seven mass-circulation dailies, I am willing to bet that no two quoted the mayor's off-the-cuff remarks exactly the same. You see, we were in the habit of doing the mayor and other interview subjects the favor of fixing their quotes. We did not change the meaning of what they said—we just improved their grammar and syntax, making it seem they were speaking better English. While some papers, like the *New York Times*, did not fix hizzoner's quotes, the rest of us did it with barely a second thought. This habit of journalists fixing grammar makes me wonder how many of our presidents over the years have shared George W. Bush's syntactical indifference only to have been rescued for posterity by journalistic grammarians.

Today, journalists and reporters no longer fix an interview subject's butchered language. The responsible party is the same beast that slew all those New York newspapers: television. As my print colleagues and I saw fewer of our number and more TV crews at news conferences, we also saw the light of truth—or the light of the dead-on accurate quote. I couldn't very well fix Mayor Wagner's quote in the *World-Telegram and Sun* if my reader was going to put down the paper, turn on the television, and hear the tortured original for himself. Television made honest men and women of us all, much to the dismay of many intelligent people who get flustered and shaken and turn into grammatical dunces during an interview.

The wording of your quotes in print interviews today is totally in your hands, so you should make every effort to speak clearly, grammatically, and in complete sentences. The most fixing a reporter might do is to add words you've omitted and enclose them in brackets. But today's print reporters won't do you the favor we used to do Mayor Wagner, of quoting you as saying what you would have said had you said it correctly.

It's more important to speak grammatically and in complete sentences for print media than it is for broadcast. Broadcasters are not as likely to toss out a grammatically fouled-up soundbite as are print reporters. There are two reasons for this. First, broadcasting needs soundbites, even if they are imperfect. If a broadcast reporter paraphrases everything an interview subject says, the story will look and sound boring; it will be a monologue. It may be gratifying to the reporter to have his face on camera for a longer time, but even the most ego-driven knows it's ultimately not good for his career to hog the screen. So broadcast journalists will cut you more slack and use an almost-grammatical soundbite before the print press will, just for the sake of getting another voice in the story. Second, broadcasting is just not as discriminating about proper English.

Nearly half a century ago, John Hohenberg, a professor at Columbia's School of Journalism, used to rail, "Broadcast copy is bad copy." If you listen carefully to what's being said and read on radio and television today, you'll be forced to agree. A good deal of what the radio and television reporters are saying is grammatically incorrect. This is

especially true when they are speaking off-the-cuff. But the casual attitude toward grammar extends to the written material as well. If you had
the opportunity to read most radio and television news scripts, you
would be amazed to find they are rife with incomplete sentences and
sloppy syntax. "More than" routinely becomes "over" in television and
radio news scripts, as in "He worked for the team for over thirty years"
instead of the grammatically correct "He worked for the team for more
than thirty years." On television, things are said to be "real good"
instead of "really good." The difference between "lay" and "lie" seems
to matter little, too. Why are radio and television scripts so cavalier
about language? Because they are written for the ear, not the eye. So in
the grammatical skid row of broadcasting, the fact that your soundbite
is a bit ragged and grammatically wanting doesn't particularly stand out.
On the other hand, readers of newspapers and magazines see your syn-
tactically challenged quote surrounded by prose that has been written
and edited in conformity to the rules of grammar. Because of this, a
print reporter is less likely than a broadcaster to use a really badly con-
structed direct quote, preferring instead to paraphrase you.

It's also a good idea to include the sense of the question in your
answer. By that I mean, if you are asked something as simple as, "How's
the weather?" instead of saying, "It's rainy and windy," say, "The
weather is rainy and windy." While "It's rainy and windy" is a complete
sentence, it isn't as quoteworthy as the sentence that incorporates the
sense of the question, because it requires the writer or TV reporter to
set up the quote. Instead of doing that, the reporter is likely to paraphrase. Extending that thought to a more likely interview question, if
asked, "Can you tell me why you feel interview subjects should incorporate the sense of a question in their answer?" I could respond, "It's
important because it gives them more complete control of their quotes,
buys them a little time to think of which of their intentional message
statements they might use in response, and also makes the reporter's job
easier because she can just use the quote without having to set it up."
Or I could use the question much more effectively by answering, "My
book *How to Make the Most of Every Media Appearance* recommends
incorporating the sense of each question in answers because that gives
a spokesperson more complete control of his quotes, buys him a little

time to think of which of his intentional message statements he might use in response, and also makes the reporter's job easier because she can just use the quote without having to set it up."

Subjectivity and Objectivity

Print is at once the most subjective and objective medium. As a general rule, print devotes many more column inches to stories than broadcast devotes time to the same story. The exception, of course, is saturation coverage, which can be exemplified by the sort of broadcasting we saw on 9/11 or after the space shuttle *Columbia* tragedy, when broadcasters covered the stories for many days in a row. As a rule, if you were to read aloud a newspaper account of virtually any story, it would eclipse the account of the same event in a typical newscast. As an exercise, I read aloud an article in a recent *Los Angeles Times* about shelters in St. Louis being overwhelmed by a flood of newly homeless persons. It took me seven minutes to read. That's nearly a third of the editorial content of a half-hour newscast, since the editorial hole in thirty-minute newscasts is usually only twenty-two minutes. Similarly, if you set in type even a substantial television news story and printed it in newspaper-column form, its brevity would be startling—virtually no TV news stories would run more than five or six inches. This difference enables a greater amount of both objectivity and subjectivity in the print media.

The relative abundance of space that a newspaper or magazine can devote to a subject enables objectivity; there is space in a print story for all sides to be expressed and for those expressions to run long enough to be thorough explanations. If you are a spokesperson for one of those sides, the effectiveness of your advocacy is totally up to you. If you give good quotes, they'll be used, and if you don't, you'll be paraphrased. If you can make your intentional message statements relevant and telling, they'll be in the story. If you can be specific, there's room to include the specifics you cite. In the homeless shelter story, for instance, one of the reporter's sources cites by name four case histories, including one of a single mother who took to a homeless shelter because, although she had a full-time job, her rent ate up more than half her income. Ironically, her job was as a social services counselor, helping needy families find resources. That specific made the story dramatic and vivid. But it was buried midstory. Had this been a television story, it would have led the report in order to grab a viewer's attention and put a human face on the situation. Because of the need to engage viewers immediately, television producers like to build from the specific to the general. It is my guess that a local commercial television station would have done that same story as a ninety-second to two-minute piece.

In a story with several contending points of view, print is apt to give more space to the debate than broadcasting will devote time to it. If equal treatment of your idea and an opposing idea fills six inches of newspaper column, the equivalent amount of broadcast time simply wouldn't be available in a daily newscast. Additionally, because television is so dependent on images and both radio and television are so dependent on soundbites, they are less likely to run subjective opinion or analytical pieces. Usually, the pictures and soundbites are wanting in these stories so they don't make very compelling viewing or listening; subjective and analytical journalism is pretty much the province of the print media, the major exception being talk-radio commentators like Rush Limbaugh.

During the furor in the autumn of 2002 over Senate Majority Leader Trent Lott's self-destructive praise of Senator Strom Thurmond's 1948 Dixiecrat run for the presidency, we saw that repeatedly. White House spokespersons were willing to talk, but not on camera, not on the record, and not for direct attribution. So the news stories were analytical. What did we see on the nightly newscasts? Each network's White House correspondent stood on the lawn in front of the executive mansion telling us—without benefit of pictures or soundbites—what the thinking was inside the building visible over his shoulder. The lack of pictures and soundbites dictated that the stories be short. Had you set them in type and laid them into a newspaper column, they would have run only three or four inches.

Compare that with the feet and yards, perhaps miles, of column space that print reporters produced on the same story, also working without those direct quotes. This was a dramatic demonstration that newspaper and magazine writers are less reliant on direct quotes to tell a story. Sometimes, they are not reliant even on facts. In opinion pieces, for example, a writer is free to give his personal view of events, people, policies, or products. The subjectivity of the analysts and opinion writers is offset by the greater amount of space print media devote to objective reporting.

So the first thing to ask a print reporter is, "What's the purpose of this interview?" Is she seeking background for a think piece or is the interview destined for inclusion in a news story? If it's the think piece, your direct quotes will likely count for less—they may never see the light of day, save paraphrased in the reporter's words. If the interview is for a news story, your quotes count; they are the only way for you to be directly represented in the story. While you're unlikely to be directly quoted in the think piece, you can use a background interview to further your agenda even though your fingerprints (i.e., your direct quotes) won't appear. Now if you're tempted to go back to Chapter 4 and find the admonition about not giving not-for-attribution comments to a reporter, this is the exception to that rule—giving a print journalist material for an opinion column or for an analytical story.

Let's refer again to the Trent Lott story. How tough was it to ascertain President Bush's attitude about the majority leader's ouster despite the fact that the president made exactly one public statement of rebuke and, in that statement, never called for Lott to step down from the leadership? It wasn't difficult at all. Anyone who read a newspaper knew that President Bush wanted Lott out. Analysts kept writing of the White House's displeasure with Lott and the White House's desire that he step down. To read it literally, the building itself, rather than its occupants, had an opinion. But the opinion expressed was that of the building's occupants, especially its most important occupant. The information came to the analysts in not-for-attribution discussions. If you are absolutely sure that you are speaking to a reporter writing a background, opinion, or analytical piece, you can speak to him not for attribution. I have one hard-and-fast ground rule for a not-for-attribution briefing: the reporter is permitted no recording devices whatsoever except a writing implement and piece of paper. If the reporter has a tape of the discussion, it is by definition on the record and has the potential of becoming for attribution. In fact, it's virtually guaranteed that any tape will one day air or a transcription of it will be printed.

You, on the other hand, must record what you say to guard against the reporter misrepresenting your words. If she does misrepresent you, and her story comes back to haunt you with your superiors, your tape of the encounter is your only proof of what you actually did say.

Here is a case in point that involved me. When I was executive producer of "Good Morning America," *Time* magazine did a story about how our program had been beating "The Today Show" for months on end and about host David Hartman's seemingly unstoppable momentum. I was one of several show staffers and executives interviewed for that story. I was told by the reporter that I could go off the record anytime I wanted and that if I had not-for-attribution material, the source of that material would not be revealed in the article. It was an invitation to dish dirt about the show and Hartman, who, by this time, had acquired a reputation in some media of being difficult to work with. Having no intention of placing my head in a noose, I declined to go off the record or to make not-for-attribution remarks. Also, practicing what I preach, I audiotaped the interview.

When the story appeared, it contained some surprising negative comments about the interviewing prowess of the show's cohost, Joan Lunden. They were not attributed to anyone and, for all I knew, were the reporter's opinions. But television show staffs are prone to gossip, and amid the finger-pointing someone told Joan that since I had been interviewed for the piece, perhaps the negative comments about her came from me. When Joan asked me about it, I was able to put the matter to rest immediately because I had my tape of my interview, in which I had said very complimentary things about her. If I had not taped the interview, it would have been merely my word against gossip—and gossip can be a very powerful force in the absence of hard facts.

When you are preparing for a print interview, it's important to remember that the reporter doesn't really need your direct quotes, whether she's writing a news story or an analytical piece. Your exact words are icing on her cake. And while a news story without direct quotes isn't as interesting to read, we've all seen them. Help yourself and help the reporter by giving her good, usable quotes. And record every word you utter in proximity to a reporter. Her pad, pencil, and tape recorder may have been put away, but her mind is still working. So keep your recorder going until she leaves your presence.

Neither your nor her options end when she leaves. As a reporter for newspapers, I frequently called sources after my primary interview to clarify points of fact or to ask a previously unasked question. You can also follow up. As noted in Chapter 4, if you listen to your tape and discover a verbal typo, you should call her up, tell her you misspoke, and give her the correct information. Also, if you left out one of your IMSs, call back and tell her that there's another important point that her readers would likely want to know about. When you are doing this, be sure you express your point for the benefit of that WSIC (Why Should I Care) listener. If you call after the interview and just deliver a slogan or a commercial, it is unlikely to get into the article.

You should even invite a callback. If the reporter initiates the callback, then inserting your omitted IMSs is less awkward. So, before the reporter leaves the interview venue, offer her the opportunity to call you back to fact-check her story. You don't want to ask her to let you read the story before it is printed; that's like asking for the right to censor it. But an offer from you to double-check the facts as she has written them is entirely in order. On some of the more thorough publications, every assertion of fact by a reporter is checked by a separate fact-checking department. Many of these departments go into excruciating detail. However, newspapers—with their tighter deadlines and dozens of stories in each edition—do not as a rule fact-check that way; in fact, I've never known of a newspaper with a separate fact-checking department. I've worked as an executive producer at two of the three major broadcast networks, and neither of them did that sort of fact-checking by a separate department either. Researchers gathered facts before a story was written but were not handed scripts and asked to check every fact in them before they were aired. Because of the absence of fact-checkers at most publications, a good, ethical reporter may well take advantage of your offer to fact-check her story, especially if there are technical, scientific, medical, or other somewhat arcane details in it with which she may be unfamiliar. When she calls back to fact-check, you can try to work in any of your omitted IMSs.

Before you sit down to a print interview, it's a good idea to marshal as many printed facts as you can and let the reporter have them to take away with her. Photographs and other visual aids help, too. Even if the newspaper doesn't run the photograph, a picture will enable the reporter to more accurately describe what you're talking about. If you are dealing with a new product, have a sample standing by and let the reporter actually use it for herself. Sometimes that will yield a good third-person recommendation: "This reporter tried the new MP3 player and found the audio reproduction to be the equal of any CD player in a fine, high-end stereo system."

How Not to Do a Print Interview

Discussing the importance of not copping an attitude in Chapter 3, I noted an interview Martha Stewart granted the *New Yorker* in connection with the insider trading accusations against her for her sale of ImClone stock in December 2002. That interview demands some additional attention because it is a textbook case of how not to do a print interview.

First there is the timing. The controversial trade—in which Ms. Stewart sold forty thousand shares of ImClone stock for $228,000— took place on December 27, 2002. The sale came one day after ImClone's chief executive, Sam Waksal, learned the Food and Drug Administration was going to reject a drug the company had developed. Waksal, who immediately began unloading his shares of ImClone, spoke with Martha Stewart—an old friend—before Ms. Stewart's stock sale. For his part, Waksal agreed to plead guilty to insider trading, so much could be—and was—made by the media of the Waksal-Stewart phone call that preceded Ms. Stewart's stock sale.

As for the timing of the *New Yorker* article, the Waksal-Stewart conversation and Ms. Stewart's sale of stock came just after Christmas 2002, on December 26 and 27. The controversy erupted almost immediately. But Ms. Stewart did not speak to the *New Yorker*'s legal correspondent, Jeffrey Toobin, until sometime in mid- to late January. Toobin's thorough and well-written article appeared in the magazine's February 3 edition—more than a month after the controversial stock trade. In the weeks between the trade and the publication of the article, the media were free to speculate about the case with virtually no input whatsoever from Martha Stewart—and speculate they did. That speculation did great damage to Ms. Stewart's cause and to her finances. In the *New Yorker* article, Ms. Stewart indicated that the cost to her personally from lost business, depressed value of her company's shares, and legal fees totaled $400 million.

So her delay—not getting out in front of the story early on—was a big mistake. It looked as if Martha Stewart had been indifferent to public opinion and felt no need to address the charges in the media, whereas her accusers were not at all reluctant to go public. In fact, Ms. Stewart did have one previous brief brush with a reporter; she had been questioned about the case by CBS News correspondent Jill Clayson during one of the domestic diva's regularly scheduled live appearances on "The Early Show." This happened immediately after the charges surfaced, and Ms. Stewart responded to Ms. Clayson by saying that everything would turn out all right and she wasn't there to discuss the charges but to do a cooking segment. Chef's knife in hand and looking annoyed, Ms. Stewart resolutely continued chopping a cabbage with great vigor. Among those who saw the episode there was an impression that she was ducking the issue. In fact, the cooking–no comment segment became fodder for late-night comedians. CBS wisely discontinued Ms. Stewart's appearances on "The Early Show" after that.

A good rule of thumb on a story likely to become controversial is to get out in public early, even if you are able to say very little. A more media-savvy move for Ms. Stewart might have been to take advantage of the CBS appearance to indicate that to avoid any negative impressions she was donating the stock sale proceeds to a charity. If such a virtual mea culpa ran counter to advice from her legal counsel, she could have resorted to saying, "This could become a legal case and attorneys advise their clients not to discuss a pending legal matter. But I can tell you I want to put even the perception of any wrongdoing behind me, so I'm donating the profits from the sale of that stock to charity." The cost of the donation would have been minuscule compared with the financial damage Ms. Stewart reported to Toobin. Also, if there were shades of gray in the case, regulators might have been more inclined to cut some slack to a public figure who had expressed remorse and rid herself of any profits from her alleged wrongdoing. The media, certainly, would have been much harder-pressed to crusade against a caring and open Martha Stewart than against a seemingly evasive and indifferent Martha Stewart.

Ms. Stewart's second mistake in her *New Yorker* interview was going off the record. It is clear from even a casual reading of Toobin's article that she is the source of some of the assertions that buttress her side of the argument. In fact, Toobin writes at the beginning of his piece that Ms. Stewart agreed to talk with him about her feelings, but that she declined to discuss the facts of the case on the record—an indication that she did discuss the facts of the case, but did so off the record. Had she not addressed the facts at all, it is likely that Toobin would have noted that instead of noting she declined to discuss them on the record.

Her third mistake was to have her IMSs right there in front of her where her interviewer could see them. Toobin reports that she had a pad in front of her with points she wanted to get into the interview. Having your notes in front of you invites the journalist to tell his readers just that—that you had your notes in front of you. Surely, Ms. Stewart, an accomplished and extraordinarily bright woman, could have memorized those points.

Ms. Stewart's fourth mistake was inviting Toobin to do the interview in her home, a restored early-nineteenth-century farmhouse. That was probably a calculated risk, but it did not pay off because part of the piece was a house tour and animal census and neither furthered Ms. Stewart's cause. While Toobin didn't ridicule the attention to detail at Ms. Stewart's house, most of us would consider the lengths to which she has gone to create her world to be ludicrous. Among those lengths were custom-tailored fabric frost covers cut to the individual shape of each outdoor shrub. Toobin mentions them without sarcasm; the readers certainly can supply that emotion without prompting by the writer. The house itself "reads" like some sort of stage set, with Ms. Stewart attended by a substantial staff of spin doctors and domestic help. This serves to distance Ms. Stewart from the public she is trying to court.

The title of Toobin's piece is "Lunch at Martha's," although the interview appears to have begun before lunch and run through the meal and extended after it. As indicated in Chapter 4, a meal is a meal and an interview is an interview, and the two should not be mixed. The normal pitfalls of a mealtime interview—interruptions by servers and the distraction of food—were exacerbated when Ms. Stewart spontaneously gave Toobin the recipe for one of the dishes they were having and insisted he write it down. At that point, without Toobin's adding any nuance to his account, Ms. Stewart descends to the depths of self-parody.

Another unfortunate moment for Ms. Stewart's cause arose at their Chinese luncheon feast when she pointed out to Toobin that in Chinese society, the higher one's social class is, the thinner one's chopsticks are. She then announced that she had sought out and purchased the thinnest chopsticks she could find. And then she added: "That's why people hate me."

Much of the interview is filled with that thin-chopstick sensibility. Ms. Stewart's attitude was so manifestly self-absorbed and so indifferent to the public that she emerged in the piece looking worse than if she had not done the interview at all. She certainly failed in her attempt to rally public sympathy for her plight. She had not merely ignored the WSIC listener, but actively alienated him.

Print interviews are a great opportunity for expressing your IMSs. They tend to be thorough, the print media tend to print longer stories, and because there is that reread factor, your ultimate audience has a chance to study and absorb your messages. Online interviews afford you similar opportunities.

Online Interviews

Online interviews fall into two categories. The first are interviews for online publications, such as the mass-appeal *Slate* or more narrowly focused online journals of various industries and disciplines. The second are scheduled sessions in online chat rooms—where the questioners are not journalists but rather journalism's end users, the audience. This is the closest most spokespersons get to dealing one-on-one with the audience they try to reach through interviews with journalists.

In the former, the interview is likely to be conducted by conventional means—on the phone or in person—by a writer who will mold what you say into a story, much the way a print journalist would. One major difference is that some online journals are more likely than their print counterparts to run the entire Q&A session in addition to the written story. Most of the interviews will likely be conducted over the phone or through the Internet equivalent, an exchange of instant messages. In either case, you can have your intentional message statements right in front of you to use as a reference. In an E-mail or instant message interview, you enjoy the additional advantage of being able to delay your responses because as "instant" as an instant message is, it's nowhere near as instantaneous as the give-and-take of a live phone conversation. You can buy yourself far more thinking time on the Internet than in person or on the phone. For an instant message or E-mail interview, you can have your IMSs open on your computer in a word-processing program and simply cut and paste them into your E-mailed responses.

A number of conventional media outlets use their websites to run longer versions of their published or broadcast stories. This is all to your advantage because while the print or broadcast news report may have had the shorter form of your IMSs, the Internet version may have full explanations, links to sites you've recommended, and other supporting material that would not fit in the article or broadcast. The only downside is that fewer people will see the Internet version. The upside is that those who take the time and trouble to look it up are the people most interested in the subject.

Chat Rooms

Internet chats more often than not appeal to an audience that is already interested in your subject and is curious to know more. Again, you can and should have your IMSs right there in front of you on your computer, available to be cut and pasted into your responses. Be sure to refer the chat participants to websites that support your point of view.

Operating in the safe anonymity of the Internet, some chat room participants throw caution and manners to the wind. Don't be caught off guard by a hostile and intemperate online attack. You are in control as long as you have your intentional message statements at hand.

The chat room is the Internet's equivalent of a radio call-in show. The big difference is that there's no interlocutor on the Internet, as there is on a radio show. Radio, the first electronic medium, offers additional challenges and opportunities as well. Radio requires some specialized tools and skills; we'll deal with the medium's unique challenges and opportunities in the next chapter.

Whether you are being interviewed for a cyber journal or the *Wall Street Journal*, the key rules are the same: prepare your points, inform yourself about whom you're really addressing, fashion quoteworthy statements, practice working your points into an interview, and don't cop an attitude, lie, or evade. Very few interviews will appear to be daunting experiences if you have your own agenda and are prepared to employ the skill set you've learned here to prosecute that agenda.

CHAPTER 9

YOU'RE ON THE AIR:
RADIO AND TELEPHONE INTERVIEWS

In 1968 when I first went to work at ABC News, the division had a prodigious radio news operation, staffed by highly professional and dedicated men and women. ABC News had divided its many radio affiliates into four mini-networks, and so the operation churned out four newscasts an hour, twenty-four hours a day, seven days a week. ABC Radio News tailored its four newscasts to different types of radio stations, ranging from the quick-paced, hip, and contemporary to the more serious information outlets. This huge operation was overseen by a jolly beardless Santa Claus of a man named Tom O'Brien, who had a big, booming radio voice and a devotion to the medium that bordered on the religious. Tom saw to it that all the ABC News television stars contributed reports to his radio networks. ABC Radio News was committing some really serious journalism.

When I became executive producer of "Good Morning America," my office had the traditional three silent TV sets monitoring ABC, CBS, and NBC, but I also had installed an ABC News radio line. I used the radio speaker several times each day, turning up the volume at any quarter hour to hear a good, professional summary of the latest top news.

Summary is the key here. Those broadcasts were highly compressed news, requiring shorter stories and briefer soundbites than even television news. Hourly radio newscasts remain to this day short form journalism, but now a distressing number of stations do no newscasts at all. Information and talk stations are at the other end of the spectrum; many feature long interviews and expansive, detailed stories that can rival in content a medium-length newspaper article.

National Public Radio's "Morning Edition" and the evening drive-time "All Things Considered" are two shows that come to mind when I look for all that's best in the radio medium. But even the newscasts on these shows on the hour and half hour are short form journalism. All-news radio stations churn out news twenty-four hours a day, but their stock in trade is the short, headline-style story, not the in-depth piece featuring substantial explanations, comprehensive soundbites, and contemplative analysis. Their news pieces normally feature extremely short soundbites and bulletin treatment of most stories. Also, all-news stations present a lot of repetition of stories, no doubt because they know there is a substantial audience "churn," with listeners tuning in and out for short bursts of information. That said, the all-news stations are voracious consumers of content and need a lot of material to stuff that 24/7 pipeline. If you are going to be part of the stuffing, your remarks need to be extremely concise and pithy.

Radio Interviews

Too many spokespersons fail to differentiate between the broadcast media. While radio shares some similarities with television, the differences require some attention.

Radio Is Not Television with the Picture Turned Off

Let's deal with the fundamentals that all radio news interviews share: no pictures and no reread factor. Radio is unlike any other medium because it is the only one that offers its audience no visual clues or cues at all. In a radio interview you have your words and nothing else. The listener can't see your sarcastic smile, your raised eyebrow, your happy grin. You are a disembodied voice.

As with television, what the listener hears—the first time—is what she takes away. She absorbs what she can as it comes her way; there is no going back to reconsider something you said earlier. So it's up to you to enable comprehension the first time around by speaking to the WSIC (Why Should I Care) listener and by making your soundbites accessible and comprehensible.

It is a rule of media mastery that you speak clearly, simply, and in short but complete sentences. Nowhere is that rule as critical as it is in radio. And add another mandate: the need to speak slowly enough that your words can be heard and comprehended.

Energy Is Radio's Equivalent of Television's Pictures

Speaking slowly does not mean speaking listlessly. On radio, you should—no, you must—energize your voice and give it character and color. You have only that one tool—your voice—to command the listener's attention. Make your voice commanding by using inflection and stresses, not by talking with machine-gun speed. You can sound energetic while still speaking slowly enough for even the most preoccupied listener to absorb what you're saying. A lot of radio personalities achieve vocal energy by acting as they speak or read. That is, they grimace and gesticulate with exaggerated movement. To brighten their speech, they do something old radio pros call "putting teeth in it." Putting teeth in a line means delivering it with a huge smile on your face. It looks ridiculous but sounds great. And, since it's not on television, no one sees your jack-o'-lantern grin. Try it. Record yourself on audiotape reading a line with normal facial expressions, and then reread it with a big smile on your face. When you play back the tape, your ears will "see" that smile.

A large number of stations, especially on the AM band, have initiated all-talk formats. There are sports talk-radio stations, political talk-radio stations, business talk-radio stations, and general informational radio stations.

The trade publications call the talk-radio stations "yakkers." Many of the yakkers employ talk jockies who, despite their high incomes and relatively easy jobs, always seem angry about something. Moreover, these angry talk jockeys draw audiences whose members are even angrier. The only thing these listeners like better than a heated argument is a verbal assault by their favorite gab jock on someone with whom they disagree. For our purposes, talk falls into two categories:

the listener-interrupted monologue and the listener-participation interview. In the former, the host delivers a commentary on the day's events and fields questions and comments from listeners. These shows rarely have guests and infrequently do interviews. Usually on the listener-participation interview shows, the guest is grilled by the host, who then throws the questioning open to the audience. An upside of these shows is the length of time they accord a guest. Frequently, there is only one booking in the show—or one subject with several guests booked—so there's really a lot of time to expound your views. The downside is that these shows are looking for action, drama, conflict, and a good argument. There's nothing like hysterically shouting opponents to attract and hold an audience.

An acquaintance of mine used to host a show of the former variety—host and callers—in Los Angeles. One day when she was contending with an obviously drunken and barely coherent caller, I phoned the station to put in my two cents. My acquaintance liked to let callers argue with each other on her show, so she put me on with the fumbling drunk. I forget the issue, but it was a then-current political hot button. I began by passionately and angrily espousing the conservative side of the argument—in opposition to the alcohol-addled caller. Midway through, I switched sides and just as passionately and angrily took the liberal side. I was, in effect, arguing with myself, and it was great good fun, probably entertaining radio, and not at all illuminating. I tell you this story because it is possible on this sort of radio show to "book" yourself some airtime by simply phoning in. But don't do as I did; don't phone in just for the entertainment value. Phone in only if you've got good, valid, prepared message points you want to make. And if you are put on the air, remember to make your points as early and as quickly as possible. The hosts of these shows normally permit a caller a single statement, which they may follow up with one or two questions—or challenges. You can't go into one of these situations expecting to leave behind four or five IMSs, but there's no reason why you can't slip in one or even two. And remember to be prepared to do all the branding yourself: "I work for Ynot Corporation, and we're totally in support of . . ."

On that type of call-in show, where the premium on conflict is so high, the value placed on full and complete discussion is minimal. Radio programs that book guests—as opposed to phone-in shows—will allow you to go on for a far greater length of time, but be aware that before going on the show, you need to ascertain to whom you're speaking and through whom you're speaking. Of all media, that information is most critical with talk-radio programs because it is so easy to get sandbagged by the host and audience of a show you don't know. So when a radio station calls to book you, it's critical to find out whether you're going to be praised, fawned over, skewered, belittled, ridiculed, or assaulted. That information is key to your preparation. If you can't listen to a radio broadcast before being interviewed, ask around and find someone who has listened to it so you can prepare for what's coming. Not all these radio shows are audio replays of the Spanish Inquisition. Indeed, some are comparable to fan magazines, with host and listeners in turn praising every guest. But at the other end of the spectrum are some very tough hosts who enjoy the loyalty of very hostile listeners.

Your principal defense against an anticipated onslaught of ridicule is your inalienable right to not do the interview. As noted earlier, no media outlet has subpoena power; you cannot be compelled to submit to an interview. If you are virtually certain that you are going to be subjected to unreasonable treatment, that you are not going to be permitted to make any points, that you are being booked only to be the object of ridicule and the target of scorn, decline the invitation to do the show— or if you've already been booked, unbook yourself. Declining an invitation is easy; virtually all talk radio is live, so it's understandable if you have a conflicting appointment that prevents you from accepting an invitation to your own public beheading. In cases where you accept an invitation and then learn enough about the show to know you're going to be skewered, unbook yourself as early as possible so the show can find a replacement in plenty of time and will not harbor any resentment against you. There are any number of perfectly reasonable excuses for retracting an acceptance to appear: appointment conflicts, legal counsel recommendation, company or organization policy. While a television station might stage a dramatic confrontation between an opponent of yours and an empty chair meant to represent you, this doesn't work on radio. The worst that can happen is the talk jock will mention once or twice that you had accepted an invitation to appear and then changed your mind. After only a couple of repetitions, this begins to sound petty and it's likely the talk jock will abandon the theme and move on to someone who is in the studio and available to be assaulted with a barrage of deadly questions.

Of course, if you are the sort of person who feels any publicity, no matter how adverse, is better than no publicity, go ahead and stick your neck out. You may win; you may not. In fact, by your own standards you may win even if a lot of listeners feel you've lost. When the Howard Stern radio show debuted in the Los Angeles market in the 1980s, I listened to the inaugural broadcast. Exercise guru Richard Simmons called in to congratulate Stern on his West Coast debut. Stern lashed into Simmons and kept up a stream of hateful invective for what seemed like a cruel eternity. I remember thinking, "Hang up, Richard. Cut it off." But Simmons stayed the course, although Stern had reduced him to tears. At the time, I was supervising producer of ABC-TV's "Home Show" and Richard was a frequent guest on the show. When I next saw him, I told him I had heard the broadcast and felt he'd been treated terribly by Stern. "Oh," said Richard, "he always does that when I'm on his show." Always? This had happened before and Richard had come back for more? To Richard Simmons, the humiliation was likely worth it because it gave him an opportunity to reach out to the overweight among Stern's listeners.

Talk-Radio Preparation

Once you make up your mind to accept an invitation to appear on a radio talk show, find out the circumstances of your appearance. Ask if you'll be the only guest and how long your segment is scheduled to be. Ask how long you'll be talking with the host before listener calls are accepted. Armed with that knowledge, try to get all of your IMSs into the host's interview before the phones are opened to the public. If you can manage that, you will have set the agenda, and the callers will be more likely to address your points with their questions and comments. Once the calls start coming in, remember to keep your points at the forefront. Often callers don't ask questions but use their time on the air to make statements. If a caller agrees with you, endorses what you said, or praises you, thank him and reiterate the point to reinforce it. This is not the time for saying, "Aw shucks, thanks a lot, caller." It's a time to put your message in audio boldface. If the caller's statement is in opposition to one of your points, we have a three-step variation on our four-step technique for answering a journalist's off-agenda question. Our original question-bridging technique along with the equivalent response to a caller statement are as follows:

Off-Point Journalist Question	*Tough or Hostile Phone-In Statement*
Give a short form answer.	Disagree at once.
Build a bridge.	State your IMS.
State your IMS.	Shut up.
Shut up.	There is no step 4.

Disagree at Once

You were not asked a question; instead, you were presented with a statement, so you don't have to feign an answer. By saying simply, "I disagree with that," you are both answering the statement and building the equivalent of a bridge. "You're dead wrong" is even stronger than "I disagree," and in the rough-and-tumble world of talk radio, you may want to be extremely assertive.

State Your IMS

You'll want to do this forcefully and quickly. Don't spend time responding to the caller's point; that just muddies the water and gives his point of view more airtime. Get your point into the listeners' ears as early in your response as possible. By doing this you are resetting the agenda from the caller's to your own. If the host is on the caller's side, he may try to shoehorn in a question sympathetic to the caller's point of view. If he does, then use that question to bridge to another of your intentional message statements.

Shut Up

In an interview setting, the final rule was to shut up—that is, to not bring your answer back to the interviewer's question, as in, "So that's why this is not a disaster waiting to happen." In response to a statement from a radio caller, you want to do the same thing; you want to end your statement on your message point, not return to his. So deliver your IMS and shut up.

Let's demonstrate this technique with something truly controversial: Ynot Corporation's plan to build a nuclear-fueled electric generating plant in the Jersey Meadowlands, just outside New York City. This, obviously, is going to be a tough sell. You have worked up four intentional message statements:

1. **The plant will be nonpolluting.** Unlike coal- and oil-fired plants, nuclear power plants emit no soot, ash, or other particulates.
2. **The plant will lessen U.S. dependence on foreign sources of energy.** At current import prices, an oil-fired plant producing the same amount of electricity would require paying overseas oil suppliers more than $200 million every year.
3. **The plant will be safe to the point of being foolproof.** The technology used in this plant has been proven over a forty-year period by nuclear-powered U.S. Navy vessels.
4. **The plant will save consumers money.** The newest technological developments mean that nuclear-generated electricity is now cheaper than electricity produced by conventionally fueled plants.

Despite your positive messages, this is going to be an emotional issue. People remember Chernobyl, the Soviet nuclear plant that melted down and released lethal levels of radioactivity in 1986. In addition, they have a fear-provoking example closer to home: Three Mile Island, which the media and nuclear critics portrayed as an American Chernobyl, although there was no significant release of radioactive material at the plant. Because this is a hot-button issue, you have armed yourself with hard facts and figures: the difference between the poorly engineered Chernobyl plant and American designs, the fact that no one was harmed at Three Mile Island, the number of U.S. Navy ships powered by nuclear reactors, the fact that France safely generates most of its electricity using nuclear reactors, and the U.S. Department of Energy's excellent record for guarding spent nuclear waste against terrorists and other potential thieves.

You're on a radio call-in show. The host has grilled you for a while, but the phones are flashing because you're dealing with such an emotional matter, so he's going to take listener calls. In a heated and emotional tone, the first caller says, "No one's going to put a nuclear power plant in my backyard. If the government's not willing to stop them, I'll go to court with my neighbors. And if that fails, we'll lie down on the highway and block the construction trucks. You're proposing exposing my kids to dangerous radioactivity." Now you're going to employ the "Disagree at Once, State Your IMS, Shut Up" technique for responding. The most logical message to work in here is your third IMS: the plant will be safe to the point of being foolproof.

There was no question, just a frightened and pugnacious statement. Here's a response using our three-step technique: "That's not the case at all. [disagree at once—without repeating the caller's point of view] Safety is our number one priority. That's why this plant has been designed to be safe to the point of being foolproof. As a matter of fact, this technology has been used safely and successfully aboard more than four hundred U.S. Navy ships over the last forty years. There has never been a nuclear mishap aboard one of those vessels in all that time, and we know this plant—built using the knowledge gained aboard those ships—will be just as safe for both workers and neighbors. [state your IMS and shut up]" By using this technique, you have not gotten bogged down in a discussion of the caller's children's safety and you've made your case in less than thirty seconds.

Radio Sins Versus Radio Virtues

Let's say you've been approached to do a radio interview by a station and talent you are reasonably sure will not assault you with a constant barrage of deadly questions and will permit you to get in your points during a vigorous but fundamentally fair interrogation. You want to emerge from the experience a radio saint, not a radio sinner. Here are the four deadly radio sins and their corresponding virtues:

Sin	*Virtue*
loquacity	brevity
silence	energy
complexity	simplicity
brand aversion	branding

Loquacity Versus Brevity

In Chapter 4 we talked about the need to keep your interview answers short and simple. Let's deal with the short part first. You already know that radio is a nonvisual medium without a reread factor. A very long statement can sound like a speech or a sermon, rather than a conversation. It is much more interesting for a listener to eavesdrop on a conversation than it is to listen to a speech. In a tough interview, many of us have an impulse to filibuster, reasoning, "If I keep talking, he can't ask me more questions." Well, speaking at excessive length may not forestall other questions and you are likely to frustrate your listeners. Once an answer has gone on too long, most radio interviewers will throw their manners to the wind in order to rescue their show and will interrupt you with their next question—which will only highlight your tactic for listeners. Even if the interviewer doesn't interrupt you, it's a safe bet that somewhere along the line in a long answer you're going to lose the attention of the listeners. So speak in short sentences and short paragraphs: one thought to a sentence and, in general, only one IMS to an answer. Brevity is not "Yes" and "No." I've already said that "Yes" and "No" are not answers but are rather the beginning of answers. A few days ago I heard an interview with a young rock musician on a local Los Angeles radio station. He was asked a question and answered, "Yes." There was the briefest of pauses, as the DJ waited for amplification. When none was forthcoming, the DJ asked a second question and got a second "Yes." Again, nothing beyond the single syllable. So the DJ did what any radio broadcaster would do in such a situation: he asked and answered the questions, pausing only for the young rocker to agree with his inevitable "Yes." Fortunately for the rocker, the DJ mentioned the name of his new CD; otherwise listeners would never have known it. Listening to an interview like this, you can be forgiven for wondering if it is a comedy routine or a genuine interview. In the case I'm citing, it was an interview—and to a certain extent, an inadvertent comedy skit.

Silence Versus Energy

Just as nature abhors a vacuum, so radio abhors silence. Think about this: if you were channel surfing on television and tuned to channel five and there was nothing on-screen—no picture, no sound—you'd move on to another channel. If you were in a strange town, you'd assume that was an empty channel with no station assigned to it. Someone hunting through the radio dial and hearing no talk, no music, just the "sound of silence" assumes that there's no station and moves on. Radio interviewers know this and don't want to lose the station surfers, so if you are silent for too long after being asked a question, it's likely your interviewer will begin talking to fill the void. When he's talking, he's using the medium's most precious commodity—airtime—and you are not. You can't deliver your message when he's talking.

Even as you remember the danger of silence, keep in mind the first deadly sin, loquacity. You want to talk, but not forever. The virtue I've paired with silence is energy. We've already talked a little bit about the need to make your voice interesting because in radio there are no supporting visuals. An energetic voice is an interesting voice. Your energy conveys enthusiasm for your intentional message statements. But don't confuse energy with speaking quickly. An energetic voice is one with coloration, emphasis, brightness—vocal qualities—not speed. Listen to the really good radio communicators: they stress words a little unnaturally for everyday conversation, they change the pace of their delivery, and they vary their volume, raising it slightly to put in boldface the words or phrases they want to emphasize. I was in the audio booth one day while Howard Cosell did his two minutes on "Good Morning America," and I watched the volume needles as they did a wild dance. Cosell would speak very quietly and then suddenly raise his voice for emphasis. His pace, too, would vary from very slow to moderately fast—but never so fast that you couldn't catch the words. Known for his television appearances, Cosell—like most sports booth announcers—was really an audio, not a visual, performer, and he made wonderful use of color and energy to make his voice interesting. He didn't have the resonant bass often associated with radio voices, but he used his reedy, nasal voice as well as anyone in the medium. So you don't have to sound like James Earl Jones to interest a radio listener. While it takes a lot of practice to get to a career announcer's stage of professionalism, you can do what they do on a more modest scale by varying your tone and your speed, by gesturing in an exaggerated way, and by "coloring" your voice by "putting teeth" into your words from time to time.

Complexity Versus Simplicity

With no reread factor as there is in print and no graphics to assist as there are in television, radio listeners get one brief shot at comprehending what you're saying. In media-training sessions I used to tell participants that rather than dumb down their answers, they should just pretend to be talking to their friend or relative across the table at Thanksgiving dinner and speak at the appropriate level for that person to understand. In Chapter 3, I told Kerry Millerick's story about being chastised for writing copy with a twelve-year-old audience in mind when, according to his producer, he should have been writing for five-year-olds. I must disagree. The danger of making things too simple is you'll insult your audience. If you speak to them as if they're five years old, you risk turning them off. Simplicity is not necessarily dumbing down what you say; it's just making sure that the audience has an opportunity to grasp what you say. That means simplifying as much as you can without changing the meaning of what you're saying. During my years at "Good Morning America," we had an arrangement with the writer Isaac Asimov. Anytime a guest didn't show up for an interview, we called on Asimov, who lived directly across the street from the studio. A prolific writer, Asimov wrote an amazing total of five hundred books before his death in 1992, so whenever we called on him at the last minute—usually about half an hour before he was to go on the air— he had something new to talk about. Known for an impressive series of science fiction books, Asimov was also a great popularizer of science fact, and many of his books shed light on scientific mysteries for the general public. To me he was always at the top of his game when he was able to make comprehensible to our audience a complex scientific theory or development. He kept it simple, but he never talked down to our viewers. He explained in layman's terms, using examples whenever possible and speaking without condescending and without showing off. That's the secret of simplicity.

Brand Aversion Versus Branding

Just before I began writing this chapter, I listened to a radio interview with a British female pop singer. Like many listeners, I joined while the show was in progress. During the portion of the interview I heard—a good three or four minutes—neither she nor the interviewer ever identified her or her band, although both made reference to "the band." Nor did either of them name her album, missing every opportunity to tell listeners what they were discussing. At one point the interviewer said, "When your CD is issued in this country there are going to be two or three additional tracks on it that weren't on the British original." (How much effort would it have been to insert the name of the CD in that statement?) "That's right," Ms. Unknown said, missing an opportunity to correct the interviewer's omission. "I'm very excited about it because when they cut one of those songs out of the U.K. version I sat down and cried because it was my favorite of all the songs we recorded." It may have been her favorite, but she failed to name it. To add to a listener's frustration, after Ms. Unknown told that story, the DJ said, "Let's listen to it," and then played the still-unidentified song on the unidentified CD by the still-unnamed artist. "That's great," he said at the end, giving a strong third-party endorsement to a product the listener could not identify. "Why, thank you," she said. Now, if I had liked that song and wanted to run out to the Virgin Megastore and buy the CD, I would have certainly stymied the clerk by asking for "that new album by a British woman with a song on it that wasn't on the original U.K. release." But that was all the identification I could muster from the interview.

It is the job of the radio interviewer to identify her interview subject for her listeners. A good radio interviewer does that with regularity—every third or fourth question. Watch Larry King's interview program on CNN and you'll see what I mean. King's many years of radio expe-rience—and the fact that his interview show is also broadcast on radio—lead him to use the guest's name in questions and to always say upon returning from a commercial, "We're talking with Senator Goodhue of South Carolina." While Larry King is without a doubt the best radio interviewer on television, watching a radio interviewer can be a little strange. "Why," you ask yourself, "is Larry King constantly using Colin Powell's name? I know the secretary of state on sight, and his name is superimposed on the screen under his face with regularity. Why the redundancy?" Because that's the way a good radio interviewer keeps his viewless audience from becoming clueless as well. A good radio inter-viewer will also help you brand. He'll not only give your name but also mention why you're on the air. Terry Gross on NPR's "Fresh Air" will say, "We're talking with George Merlis, author of *How to Make the Most of Every Media Appearance*," from time to time. And she'll ask questions like this: "George Merlis, in your book *How to Make the Most of Every Media Appearance* you contend that it's up to the guest to mention his brand during an interview. Why is that necessary?" But not every inter-viewer is that professional or conscientious, so it's up to you to do that branding. For instance, to a host who doesn't use the book name, I might say, "Well, [insert name of errant interviewer], my book *How to Make the Most of Every Media Appearance* gives readers the tools to be the best guests on your show that they can possibly be so that they help you do your job of entertaining and informing your audience." Again, my response is not, "Well, *my book* gives readers the tools . . ."

Not too long ago I was doing media training for a recording artist, who asked me, "How do I get my name in if the radio interviewer never uses it? Won't that sound egotistical?" I explained to him that it is, indeed, a lot easier to work in a band's name than a solo artist's name. "Well, our band, Wolfbite, has a unique sound" comes to the tongue a lot easier than saying, "The Frank Ritchie sound is unique because . . ." There was a tendency some years ago for some artists to speak of them-selves in the third person. I vividly remember Diana Ross on "Good Morning America" beginning the answer to a David Hartman question along these lines: "Well, that wasn't the right career move for Diana

Ross, so . . ." And throughout the interview she kept talking about herself in the third person. In the control room we joked about the identity of the Diana Ross look-alike David was interviewing. Shortly after that, I noticed that a whole raft of show business figures had begun speaking about themselves as if their entertainment persona were a separate individual altogether. Thankfully, that bizarre trend ended, although when he was running for president in 1996, Senator Bob Dole briefly revived it, talking repeatedly about "Bob Dole," as if he were discussing another person.

Since you don't want to talk about yourself in the third person, it is difficult—but not impossible—to identify yourself if a radio interviewer fails to do it for you. The easiest way to do it is to quote someone else. "You know, I was really honored when *Rolling Stone* wrote, 'Frank Ritchie is the new Elton John.'" Another way is to include yourself in a story: "I dropped my middle name, Phillip, when I was twelve and became just Frank Ritchie." Obviously, you resort to these awkward strategies only if forced to by the interviewer's failure to identify you. And you do it only on radio.

Telephone Interviews

Often a radio interview will be conducted over the phone. So, too, will many—if not most—print interviews. In a phone interview you are like the radio listener—you have no visual clues to the interviewer's attitude, expression, or demeanor. But the phone offers some unique advantages over in-person interviews, too.

A print or radio reporter sitting at his desk and working the phones can reach many different contacts in the time it might take him to travel to one venue and interview a single source. Additionally, the phoner gives the reporter the flexibility to call you, interview you, call someone else, get a different point of view on the subject, and call you back to get your reaction—setting the stage for a good, rousing conflict of quotes in his story. Even "beat" reporters use the phone extensively. A reporter assigned to Congress is more likely to phone various congressional sources for quotes and information than he is to wander the halls of the institution, knocking on doors to see sources in person. Typically, the reporters will leave their offices for hearings and for special longer interviews but will do the routine reporting by phone.

I estimate that 80 to 90 percent of the interviews I conducted during my newspaper career were phoners. I wrote hundreds of stories without ever seeing the interview subjects with whom I was dealing. I had a fair number of regular sources and contacts whom I never met in person; they were solely telephone acquaintances. I covered housing at the *World-Telegram and Sun* and spoke to the Housing Authority publicity man a dozen times before I ever met him in person. And that meeting had nothing to do with my job as a reporter; I was volunteering for a slot in the Army Reserve unit he commanded. Had I not been seeking that slot, I could have gone on for years speaking with regularity to this man without ever meeting him in person.

Be aware that the phone call from a reporter will not necessarily come to your office, nor will it necessarily be during normal business hours. You could be called at home and at extremely odd hours. Most morning newspapers "lock" their first editions after 9 or 10 P.M. Reporters seeking information on stories will work the phones right up until that deadline. On a really big story, a paper might even extend the deadline by ten or fifteen minutes. If you're a source, don't be surprised to answer a late-evening phone call and find a reporter at the other end instead of the expected telemarketer. The dwindling number of afternoon newspapers have even later deadlines for their first editions. As a reporter for the afternoon *World-Telegram and Sun*, I placed more than a few calls to news sources in their homes well after their bedtimes. Calling people at 11 P.M. or midnight for comment on a story usually yielded far more unguarded statements than I got when I called during the normal hours. It also yielded more than a few exasperated cries of "How dare you call me at this hour of the night?" This was usually followed by the slamming of a handset. When that happened, I would write, "Reached at his home, Mr. Maybury declined to comment for this story." While the vast majority of my newspaper interviews were done over the phone, none of my television interviews were ever conducted over the phone, although preinterviews—interview auditions, as

I call them—always were. You will, from time to time, "see" a television interview conducted over a phone line. Usually it involves a breaking story and the interview subject is at a location that cameras are unable to reach in time for the broadcast.

The Up- and Downsides of Phoners

Whatever the medium, the advantages of phone interviews for the reporter are obvious, and there are advantages for you as well. But there is also a downside to phoners; being interviewed over the phone can be either a blessing or a curse. Let's deal with the negative side first. Think about how we normally converse on the phone. Without eye contact, we tend to be more open, more confidential, and more revealing of our feelings than we are in face-to-face conversations. Without seeing the response of the other party to our conversation, we imagine the person's acceptance of our argument, his or her agreement with our points—why else would the person stay on the line? That assumed agreement leads to still more openness on our part. The telephonic openness to which most of us have become accustomed is a pitfall for phone interviews with the media. The fact that we're talking to a reporter using the same instrument that leads us into natural, relaxed conversation with our best friend doesn't mean the reporter has suddenly become our best friend. The telephone has a way of lulling us into a state of self-revelation, and that may lead us to stray from our agenda and casually stroll right up the gallows steps to hang ourselves with our own words.

So it's incumbent on you to be on guard when on the phone. When you talk to a reporter on the phone, you are working, not chatting. And no matter how conversational the reporter gets, she is working, too. In fact, that casual, conversational attitude she strikes on the phone is most likely just a highly refined technique she uses to get you to be more revelatory than you really want to be. That said, the very same aspect of phoners that allows you to forget you're talking to a reporter—the absence of any visual response—also allows you to use the phone to its greatest advantage.

In a phone interview you can—and should—have your intentional message statements laid out on a table or desk in front of you. If you've noticed that there is a flaw in your interview technique, you can—and should—post in your line of sight notes to yourself such as "Slow Down!" or "Give Specifics!" or "Remember Why Should I Care!" Having these cues at hand will remind you of two things: the fact that you are not having a casual chat, but are working, and the goal of that work—getting your agenda through the reporter to her readers or listeners. You are not cheating on your college geology test if you read your own intentional message statements during a phoner. They are not crib notes; they are your points. The reporter may well be reading her questions, so why not read your answers? To further guard against becoming too chatty, I encourage people to stand up and gesture broadly when they do phone interviews. That way, they can't fall into the trap of putting their feet up on the desk, letting their guard down, and saying something they'll later regret. Also, expansive gestures help you make your voice more interesting for radio interviews conducted over the phone.

Calls out of the Blue

If you get a call from a reporter out of the blue and he wants to do an interview right then and there, say "No." You need to buy yourself enough time to get organized. You also want to find out if the reporter is who he claims to be and if the story he's working on is actually the story he describes to you or if that is a cover to engage you in a conversation about something else. The "reporter" on the phone may not be a reporter at all—something you'll learn by calling back his organization. He may be a business competitor or someone else with a nonjournalistic agenda. I heard of one possibly apocryphal case where a private detective, identifying himself as a reporter, called someone in an attempt to lure him into making slanderous remarks against a particularly litigious client who was looking for grounds to file a lawsuit. You are perfectly within your rights to suggest a later time for the interview. Tell him, "I can't talk to you right now; I've got a meeting about to start. Let me call you back in two hours." If he says he's on deadline, be suspicious. Sometimes he is not on deadline at all but is saying he is because he fears you won't call back. Sometimes his deadline is self-imposed; he wants to complete his interview with you so he can call a second source and get reaction to your comments. Sometimes he simply doesn't want to wait until he actually is on deadline to write his story. For a few months when I was a reporter for the *World-Telegram and Sun*, I sat next to a reporter who was always on deadline when he called a source. It was funny to hear him tell someone at 10 A.M. that he was on deadline and then hear him tell another source he was on deadline at 4 P.M. The ploy of "I'm on deadline," by the way, almost always worked for that reporter.

If the journalist phoning you is really on deadline, he may have waited until the last minute to call you for a reason—usually so you don't have time to adequately prepare a response. This is a trick Bob Woodward and Carl Bernstein of the *Washington Post* often used during their Watergate investigation, and they chronicled that practice in their book *All the President's Men*. They would call Attorney General John Mitchell or other Nixon administration officials just prior to deadline so that there was no time for the sources to concoct a response or to do damage control. Now, this isn't to say that reporters call on deadline only with mischief in mind. Sometimes news breaks right up against a deadline, and when it does and they're trying to get comment on the breaking developments, the deadline is very real and there is no malevolence involved. You will know those instances by the circumstances of the story. If your plant sprang a leak of toxic chemicals half an hour before the local newspaper's deadline, the reporter is not playing games when he calls you and says he's on deadline. Even so, don't talk to a cold caller; call him back—even if your delay is only five or ten minutes. You need time to organize yourself and your ideas for any and every interview. Those deadline calls will frequently come to your home. Don't be surprised to get such a call even if you have an unlisted number— reporters are very adept at ferreting out unlisted numbers, cell phone numbers, and even home E-mail account addresses. Remember my experience: many of the sources who didn't angrily hang up on me late at night gave me more unguarded comments than they would have given had I reached them in their offices during business hours. So always offer to call back; it's the best way you can buy yourself some preparation time.

Once satisfactory arrangements for the interview have been made, array your IMSs in front of you, round up any additional notes you may need, invite in a witness to hear your side of the interview (to guard against misstatements), and set up your recording device. Most portable tape recorders can be equipped with a simple, inexpensive suction cup device that attaches to the handset and permits recording of both sides of the conversation. A number of home answering machines also permit recording of both sides of a phone conversation.

Call the reporter back, alert him to the fact that you're recording the interview, and tell him how much time you can devote to him ("I can give you ten minutes—I'm sure that will be adequate"). As always, if the interview is going very well, you can extend the ten minutes for as long as it suits you. But at least you've set up the ground rules and he can't write, "After being asked about the toxic spill, Mr. XYZ cut short the interview." If you're dissatisfied with the interview's progress, stick to the time limit you've announced at the outset. You'll want to put a stopwatch to the conversation so you know exactly when you can bail out if it is going poorly. With each question the reporter asks, study your IMSs and see whether the question leads logically to one of them or whether there is a relatively easy bridge you can build between a short form answer and an IMS. Again, don't be shy about reading your IMSs. He can't see you, and it's the best way of getting them into the interview. Check off each IMS as you use it so you'll be sure to get to all of them. Repeat those that are particularly important using different phrasing the second time.

My most successful experience as an interview subject came in a phone interview I gave to *TV Guide*. I quite literally read my part from a script I had written. I did not just have a list of intentional message statements; I had quips, jokes, and pithy comments, too—all of which I had written in advance. The circumstances were these: when I was executive producer of "Good Morning America," we hired and then fired as the show's gossip columnist a woman I'll call Mary Sunshine. Mary had done the best audition I'd ever seen and followed it with thirteen weeks of disappointing performance. It was as if all her talent had been expended in the audition. Additionally, Mary got distracted by the perks of her role and spent too much of her time and energy on them and not enough on gathering gossip for the show. One glaring example: she spent about two-thirds of her generous wardrobe allowance on shoes, this when she was always taped sitting behind a desk talking directly to the camera. In thirteen weeks, viewers never once saw her feet!

When ABC fired Mary, she did not go quietly into the night but told her version of this abbreviated career to *TV Guide*. The magazine saw a good conflict and hence a good story—little David (Mary) versus big, bad Goliath (ABC). As the show's executive producer, I was chosen to fill the unenviable role of Goliath's spokesperson. I knew *TV Guide* was going to go into this story with a pro-David attitude—how could they not?—so I had my work cut out for me. Knowing it was going to be an uphill battle, I sat down at my typewriter and wrote out every point I thought Mary might have made in her interview. I then wrote responses to every one of them, making those responses as quoteworthy as I could.

The *TV Guide* interviewer was in California, where Mary Sunshine was based, and I was in New York, so my interview was conducted over the phone. I had my tape recorder set up and my papers splayed out on my desk in front of me. As the interview progressed, I realized from the questions that I had nailed everything Mary had told the *TV Guide* reporter. So for each question I had not just an answer but a concise, pithy quote. When I was preparing for the interview, I had come up with one line that really pleased me, and I thought, "This one ought to be the last line of the article." When the article appeared, it was the last line: "The problem with [Mary Sunshine] was she fell in love with her limousine and forgot where it was going." It not only ended the article but also epitomized its tone. On this rare occasion, Goliath won.

I tell you this story not to pat my own back for being clever, but to show just how effective you can be by having complete message points prepared in advance and by reading them in a phone interview. Remember, the preparation is only half the assignment. Your notes are there to be read. On a number of occasions I've had media-training participants go through the exercise of preparing messages for phone interviews only to leave them sitting on the desk in front of them unread and unused. When I see them doing that I sometimes throw this question into the interview: "Aren't you going to use those great notes you've prepared?" That usually gets a laugh, but it also produces the desired response. For reasons unclear to me, some people are uncomfortable reading—or even referring to—written material during a phone interview. Get over it. Take advantage of the unique opportunity you have in a phoner; use your notes to get all your points across. All the preinterview preparation in the world is of no benefit if you don't use what you've prepared.

There's a very good reason that the first commandment of interviews is Thou shalt be prepared. Without that advance preparation, an interview is a game of chance. And media exposure is too valuable to be left to chance.

In the next chapter, we'll review another occasion where you can have your IMSs in front of you—news conferences—and deal with the unique challenges of on-camera demonstrations.

CHAPTER 10

WHEN YOU'RE IN CHARGE:
ON-CAMERA DEMONSTRATIONS AND NEWS CONFERENCES

There are two circumstances when a media encounter is specifically about your agenda and, usually, only about your agenda. These are on-camera television demonstrations conducted by a product spokesperson and news conferences. In the first instance, you have been booked solely to explain and demonstrate your product (I include as products how-to books, such as cookbooks). Therefore, the entire segment is designed to accommodate your agenda (i.e., your product), and you have far more control of the situation than you would in a conventional broadcast or print interview. In the latter, reporters and camera crews have come to the press conference at your invitation to hear the news you will make. In other words, your agenda has drawn them to the venue in the first place, so you are in charge—at least at the beginning of the news conference. (Later in this chapter, I'll show you how to remain in charge throughout the news conference or regain control should things start to get out of hand.) In any event, after reading this chapter, you'll have specific tools to help you maintain your cool and handle even the most challenging news conferences or on-camera demonstrations.

On-Camera Demonstrations

Increasingly, spokespersons are called upon to do more than just talk on television; they are asked to demonstrate. A demonstration can be something as simple as voicing-over some prepared videotape you've supplied to the program, or it may be holding up a prop and showing it to the camera. More involved demonstrations are actual how-to segments where a spokesperson may have to do something like a repair, design, technical, or food-preparation project step-by-step.

The following are tips for conducting any type of demonstrations before a camera:

Rehearse, rehearse, rehearse.
Move slowly.
Hold items steady.
Hold items for a long time.
Hold your dominant palm toward the close-up camera.
Talk while you work, but talk about the work.
Be prepared to accordion your demonstration.

Rehearse, Rehearse, Rehearse

Rehearse giving your demonstration while keeping in mind all the tips in this section and then rehearse some more. Practice doing the demonstration in different lengths of time: two minutes, three minutes, four minutes, and—you should be this lucky!—five minutes. Prepare all of your pieces, ingredients, and tools beforehand, and lay them out in a logical order so the camera follows them left to right (meaning they are right to left for you because you are facing the camera). If at all possible, rehearse on camera. If you can have only a single camera at rehearsal, have it focus on the close-ups to make sure they work. Don't worry about the wide shot; viewers get their most important information from the close-ups. Also, use a monitor so you can watch your movements as you are making them. A home video camera will work, too. Playing back a tape to critique yourself is helpful but less so than watching the action live. Don't let the monitor or tape throw you because it looks "wrong." A television image is a direct image, not a mirror image. When we lift our right hand while looking in a mirror, the hand on the right side of the mirror—as we look at it—goes up. In a television image, it is the hand on the left side of the screen that goes up. The television image is the accurate one; it is another person's view of us. But since most of us are accustomed to seeing ourselves only in a mirror, the TV monitor's image may be very disconcerting at first.

Move Slowly

Jan Rifkinson, the first "Good Morning America" director, used to say to guests who were doing demos, "Move as if you are under water," which is a sound piece of advice. Visualize how the resistance of water keeps you from making rapid movements when you're in a lake, a pool, or an ocean. That's exactly how you should move when on camera. The close-up camera has difficulty following rapid movements; you can sometimes yank items right out of the camera's frame if you move them too fast. Even if the items stay in frame, rapid movement may seem like a blur to the viewer at home.

Hold Items Steady

The close-up camera exaggerates any sort of motion, so if you hold something in a shaky or an unsteady manner, it looks awful for viewers. This is especially critical if there is anything they have to read, such as a book jacket or CD cover. The easiest way to hold items steady is to have your hands resting on the table or counter while you hold the item; the solid base on which you're resting your hands will keep them from moving. If you must hold an item up, try holding it with both hands, elbows bent ninety degrees and locked firmly against your sides. This gives your forearms and hands extra support and rigidity.

Hold Items for a Long Time

If you think you've held something in place for enough time, you're wrong. Extend the hold by at least 50 percent more time. You do this to let the camera catch up with you. If you hold up a book, a CD, or a plate of freshly prepared asparagus and take it down quickly, the camera may not have enough time to find it, frame up on it, and get into focus. Before you begin, ask to have a monitor placed in your line of sight so you can sneak a peek and make sure your item is on camera long enough to be identified. Again, remember the television monitor is a direct view, not a mirror image. If your item is off-center to the right of the screen, your instinct—having grown up looking in mirrors—will be to move it to the left. But to center it up on television, you move it to the right. It is totally counterintuitive and can be daunting to master. Camera operators will try to frame up on your item properly, and most hosts of programs featuring demonstrations are savvy about positioning of items, so they, too, usually can help. But it's much easier if you get it right so the host can concentrate on the content of the demonstration rather than on your placement of the items.

Hold Your Dominant Palm Toward the Close-Up Camera

You should stand at the demonstration counter with your elbows bent and your hands out, palms perpendicular to the counter. If you are right-handed, the close-up camera should be on your left, aimed into the palm of your right hand. If you are left-handed, the close-up camera should be on your right, shooting into the palm of your left hand. If you are wondering why, take the case of a right-handed guest doing a demonstration. If the close-up camera is shooting from his right, the back of his dominant hand is going to cover the details of the work he is doing.

It is surprising how many television directors don't know this very basic rule for shooting close-ups of demos. You can't be expected to direct your own segment, so what can you do about it? I suggest that during the run-through you ask which is the close-up camera and, if it's on the wrong side, gently point out to the director or the stage manager that you are right-handed (or left-handed) and your right (or left) hand may block the close-up camera. If there is no run-through, ask the stage manager, before you go on, which is the close-up camera. If it is on the wrong side, move even more slowly than suggested earlier and periodically take your hand away from the work so the camera can get an unobscured shot.

Talk While You Work, but Talk About the Work

As bad as directors who don't know where to place their close-up cameras are hosts who ask you questions about other matters while you are doing a demonstration. Imagine you are about to show the host how to score a mango. As you begin you state that the mango is the most popular fruit in the world, even though it is largely unknown in the United States. Picking up on the word *fruit*, she asks you whether the tomato· is a fruit or a vegetable. If you answer the question while continuing to score the mango, the viewers lose out on having you narrate while you demonstrate—the most basic element of a demonstration. The solution: stop scoring that mango while you answer the question very quickly and then segue back to the demonstration and talk about what you are doing as you do it.

Be Prepared to Accordion Your Demonstration

Before you go on, you may be told you'll have four minutes. So you go into your four-minute mode—but you're only two-thirds of the way in when the stage manager starts frantically signaling the talent to wrap it up. This happens all the time because demos often are done on live shows, and a curse of the live show is that segments after the first or second act are always being squeezed. When the talent, responding to the stage manager, says to you, "Now, moving along, how do we get to the final product?" you may well be wondering what you should do. If you had rehearsed, rehearsed, and rehearsed some more and if you had rehearsed your demonstration at various lengths, you could easily move to the shortest version of the demo for whatever steps remain. You may feel cheated, but you won't appear flustered if you have prepared for this almost inevitable eventuality.

Some of the most effective messages are delivered during demonstrations. When you're doing something, you really have the viewer's attention. Just remember that in addition to the "show" there's the "tell" element: you want to work your IMSs into your discussion of what you're doing. Practice will make you perfect at demonstrating and messaging at the same time. News conferences, too, are a great arena for expounding on your agenda.

News Conferences

A news conference is an opportunity to reach many media outlets simultaneously. But it also presents a unique set of challenges to a spokesperson. More about those in a moment; first let's consider when and why you might want to call a news conference.

A variety of circumstances demand news conferences. At some government agencies, press briefings are held daily or weekly to fill in the press corps on the activities of the agency. Companies typically hold news conferences when they announce new products, reveal major economic plans, or respond to developments either good or bad that may impact their earnings. Nonprofits often call news conferences when they announce new initiatives, new fund-raising activity, or developments that have been made possible by their efforts. In times of labor strife—or impending strife—it is not unusual for both labor and management to set out their positions before the public in a series of dueling news conferences. A news conference sends the signal that your story is more important than the ordinary grist for the reportorial mills; that it demands the news media's in-person attention; that you are putting a face on your story, setting it apart from a routine printed press release or a video news release.

Sometimes, news conferences are conducted when there is no news; they are designed simply to keep speculation and bad information from creating an inaccurate impression among the public. For instance, during the 2002 sniper attacks in the Washington, D.C., area there were daily news conferences usually conducted by Charles Moose, the police chief of Montgomery County, Maryland. At many of these sessions, Chief Moose had no real news to report, but he kept briefing the media on a regular basis to let the public know that his and other agencies were investigating the shootings and were following all leads. By conducting such a news conference, Chief Moose could also rebut speculation and dampen rumors. While reporters might grumble that there had been "no news," if the conference prevented speculation and rumor from being disseminated, it served the purposes both of the police and of journalism by keeping inaccurate information from reaching the public. On other occasions, Chief Moose used the news conferences to try to communicate with the snipers. In those instances, the conferences themselves became part of the story as well as a mechanism for covering the story.

What You Should Bring to a News Conference

The assembled press should be given supporting documentation and visuals at the news conference. If you are announcing a new product or service, thorough descriptions should be included in the handout materials. It is in these materials that the most minute and highly technical details should be laid out. Also, you should make available handout photographs, diagrams, videotape, audiotape, and even CD-ROMs to enhance your presentation. As far as videotape is concerned, you are usually better served by handing out a B-roll package—the elements a reporter can use to make a story—than by giving them an edited story. If a news conference kicks off an event, you may want to supply both background video and live pictures. Two of the most successful projects I ever did involved just that. In one instance, a Japanese auto manufacturer was about to ship to Japan the first batch of a particular model that it made only in the United States. We supplied the assembled media B-roll of the manufacture of the autos, and we covered the news conference with three cameras strategically placed, feeding via satellite live video pictures of the spokesperson's comments and of the cars rolling out of the parking lot, up a ramp, and onto the ship that would take them to Japan. Hundreds of television stations nationwide and in Japan and two U.S. network nightly newscasts used the images.

In the other instance, a fast-food restaurant destroyed by fire during rioting in the Los Angeles area was to be rebuilt from the ground up in no more than forty-eight hours. We positioned a video camera atop a neighboring building, and every ten minutes or so over the forty-two hours it actually took to rebuild the structure, we rolled off thirty seconds of video. When the building was completed, we quickly cut together a forty-two-second stop-motion animation version of the forty-two-hour build and made multiple copies for the television media attending the news conference. Then we covered the news conference live, feeding the spokesperson's announcements and the reopening of the restaurant nationwide via satellite. We rolled in the forty-two-second stop-motion animation at the end of the news conference. Again hundreds of television stations across the country and one of the major broadcast networks used our stop-motion animation.

The lesson here is you'll enhance your news conference significantly if you give the attending television outlets additional video to take away along with the printed material and still pictures. Newspapers love visuals, in the form of stills, charts, and graphs, almost as much as television. For radio, if you're dealing with a product or project that involves sound of any kind, make audiocassettes and distribute them to the radio stations that attend the news conference. You may also want to include in the cassette soundbites from persons unavailable for the actual news conference.

How News Conferences Differ from Interviews

As anyone who has watched presidential or government news conferences on live television knows, a massed press can be a lot tougher than a single reporter. In a one-on-one interview, a reporter normally asks a question and moves on. Dodge a question in a one-on-one interview and the reporter may or may not press the point. Dodge a question in front of a dozen reporters and at least a few of them will spring from their seats, waving to get your attention and put your feet back to the fire.

And that's just the beginning of the differences between a press conference and a one-on-one interview. Even if you've gotten comfortable enough with your media-mastery skills to consider an interview with a single reporter to be an opportunity, you may find a news conference, where you'll face a dozen reporters at once, daunting. After all, when you prepare for a one-on-one interview, you can bone up on the reporter's work, his leanings, and his publication. You can assess attitudes and style. But you can't do that for the dozen publications and broadcast outlets that will be sending representatives to your news conference. Before a one-on-one, your research can help you gauge the level of sophistication of the reporter's readers or listeners and you can tailor your answers to her audience. In a one-on-one, you likely will have a warm-up period, which you can use to plant seeds for questions that will serve your agenda. None of that is available to you in a news conference. You may have reporters representing the most sophisticated publications as well as representatives of supermarket tabloids. Moreover, there is scant opportunity for a warm-up—you can't very well chat up five or ten or more reporters before the formal beginning of the session.

Your news conference attendees may represent a variety of media as well. There may be television cameras, still photographers, print reporters, and radio reporters. You may be speaking into a veritable forest of microphones, and you may be facing not one or two but half a dozen bright television lights as well as the repeated blinding flashes of still cameras' strobes. Instead of the conversational tones you've come to expect from one-on-one interviewers, the reporters may shout their questions at you. Because they are in competition with each other to get their own questions asked and because they know that the amount of time available to them is finite, their manners may go by the board.

A news conference poses a host of challenges for you: How do you answer a rudely shouted question? Do you adopt the cosmetic style and posture of a television interview? Do you keep your answers simple, even though there are some pretty sophisticated and specialized media outlets represented among the reporters? How do you keep one reporter from dominating the session by asking a string of follow-up questions or making a speech? How do you end a news conference, when reporters show no signs of abating their question flow? How do you deal with redundant questions?

Despite these challenges, a news conference is an opportunity to reach many media outlets—and their readers, viewers, and listeners—

with great economy of time. And an array of simple techniques will help you maximize that opportunity.

To Whom Are You Speaking?

You might be conflicted: do you speak to the lowest common denominator or do you try to tailor each answer to the outlet represented by the reporter asking the question? Attempting the latter puts an undue burden on you. You'll have to keep changing your tone and level of sophistication throughout the news conference, and you'll have to remember to whom you're talking with each answer. If you answer for the sophisticated audience, you'll run the risk of being asked the same question over again by someone who represents an outlet appealing to the mass audience. So for a news conference, go with the basics. Oftentimes the basic answer will suffice for all the media in attendance. For example, I do a lot of work prepping scientists for news briefings. The range of reporters may run from *USA Today* to the magazine *Science*. Clearly, the readers of *Science* are a lot more sophisticated about the subject of the conference than the average reader of *USA Today*. I tell my clients to use the *USA Today* answers, and then, if the *Science* reporter needs additional information, he can usually glean it from the printed handout material that you bring to the news conference. The oral part of the news conference should be addressed to the mass audience. The supporting documents can be extremely sophisticated for those specialists who need an advanced level of detail.

Opening Remarks: You're in Control

Despite the fact that your dread of reporters may be multiplied many times over when you're facing a horde of them, remember this: if you're presiding at a news conference and if reporters are attending, they're attending because they are responding to your agenda. When announcing the conference, you or your publicity representatives informed them that you're about to make news, and that news is of sufficient interest for them to attend. You have initial control over the agenda because you've told them, usually in very general terms, what the announcement is about. The first thing you do in your news conference is make opening remarks that further set the agenda. Never begin a news conference without making an opening statement. If you don't take advantage of that opportunity, you are yielding control of the agenda right at the start.

Before the press assembles, place your opening statement and your intentional message statements on the lectern, so you'll be ready to read the former and refer to the latter during the session.

Don't read the first or last sentences of your opening remarks; deliver them from memory. If you begin by engaging the room—and not staring at the lectern—and conclude your opening the same way, you will have the attention of your audience. Make the first and last sentences of your conference opening statement assertive and quoteworthy. From the point of view of television, these are the prepared remarks most likely to be used because you won't be reading them. Make them good and strong as in this hypothetical first sentence: "Today, Ynot Corporation is announcing a major breakthrough in the production of home fuel cells—a breakthrough that we envision will allow every home in America to generate its own electricity at a fraction of the price we now pay for power and with no environmentally harmful side effects whatsoever." And, similarly, this last sentence: "The Ynot fuel cell will help lessen our dependence on foreign energy sources and significantly reduce air pollution at the same time." If you can deliver these two lines without referring to your notes, the television cameras will love you for it.

Dress the Lectern

Earlier I wrote that you should place your IMSs right there on the lectern in front of you at a news conference. An occasional glance down will refresh your memory about which one you can deploy to answer a given question, and the gesture does not look unnatural. It will look peculiar, however, if you address your answers to your IMSs on the lectern. Use them only for reference; do not read them. It's a good idea to reduce your IMSs to bullet points so you won't be tempted to read them verbatim. In addition to placing your notes on the lectern before the press files into the room, you should leave them there on the lectern at the end and have an associate collect them immediately after you leave the platform. Why plant them before you begin? I'm sure you've seen speakers approach a lectern and, as I call it, get dressed. They walk up, they fumble in a pocket—or, worse yet, in a briefcase—for their notes, they organize them, all the while looking down, they spread them out, and then they begin. They've had their eyes downcast for so long, the room may get restive. Someone approaching a lectern this way certainly does not command our attention or our confidence. A speaker who appears so dependent on his materials diminishes his credibility.

Additional News Conference Tips

Don't rest your elbows on the lectern. It looks sloppy and on television sends the wrong body language message that you need the support. Also, don't grasp the lectern. If you do, you're unlikely to use your hands to gesture. I've seen speakers hold on to the lectern as if it were a lifeboat lowered into the icy waters of the Atlantic when the *Titanic* sank. The lectern is there for your notes, not to hold up your frail being. If you want to command the news media's respect and attention, stand on your own two feet.

Dress the room correctly. How many television stories have you seen that included footage from news conferences where the only supporting visual is the name of the hotel printed on the lectern? You are not there to promote a hotel; you are there to promote a cause, a product, a position, or a policy, so bring signage to hang on the lectern and, if possible, more signage to hang behind you. It may be the corporate logo or it may be the name of the cause, product, position, or policy. Regardless, visual aids help.

It's a good idea to rehearse with stand-ins for the media—especially for television to make certain the cameras will have a good shot of you. I attended a news conference in Las Vegas where the American flag had been placed downstage of the lectern, so that the television cameras' shot of the speaker at the lectern was partially obscured by the flag. If the news conference organizers had stood on the camera platform in advance and looked at the stage, they would have realized that the flag blocked the shot. Had they done that little bit of a survey, they certainly would have moved the flag behind the lectern, where it would have supplied a patriotic backdrop instead of a distracting foreground.

At the end of your prepared statement, call for questions. You will want to set a time limit on the session. "We'll take questions for ten minutes." That puts everyone on notice that this is a Q&A session and not an invitation for reporters to begin giving their opinions. Any reporter who starts making a speech after you've given a finite length to the news conference is likely to be admonished by his colleagues. The usual line they hurl at such a colleague is, "Is there a question somewhere in the near future?" In the event you do get a speechifier and his colleagues don't shut him up, you have control of the lectern and the microphone, so pick out a question in his ramblings and answer it. "I can see you're concerned about how we will distribute these fuel cells, and let me answer that." In other words, if no question is forthcoming, infer one.

Work the Room

When making your opening statement, speak to the whole room. Start at the center, express a thought, move on to the reporters on your left, express a thought, turn your attention to the reporters on your right, and so on. Don't do a radar sweep of the room. You won't engage anyone that way. As a reporter, I've been to a number of news conferences where all remarks were addressed to a fixed spot at the back of the room. I always wanted to turn around and see whom the speaker was addressing because it certainly was never me or anyone around me. When I once asked a back-of-the-room concentrator why he was doing that, he told me, "Well, I was told to always speak to an imaginary clock on the back wall." Talk to an imaginary clock when you have warm human bodies to address? Whoever gave that bit of oratorical misinformation ought to be sentenced to a lifetime of attending speeches by people who speak to clocks on walls.

During the Q&A portion, when you're asked a question, begin your answer directly to the questioner. Then, when you've finished a thought, move to another part of the room. If the question was a friendly one, go back and end your answer looking directly at the questioner. That way, if he's got a follow-up, you're in position to recognize him. If the question was a tough one, don't go back to him at the end of your answer, so if he does have a follow-up, your attention is on another part of the room, where, hopefully, you'll get a friendlier question. In terms of taking questions, you'd be well advised to take your first question from a reporter who has treated you fairly in the past, because chances are he will again. Do not recognize for the first question someone whom you know to be a skeptical or tough questioner. Why start the Q&A portion on a negative note? Often the first question or two will set the tone for the entire Q&A portion of your news conference. Similarly, try to wrap up the Q&A on a positive note by taking your last question from another reporter who has been friendly or positive in the past.

Keep an eye on your stopwatch. If you've told the assembled media that you'll take questions for fifteen minutes, and if the conference has been tough, after thirteen minutes have elapsed announce that time's almost up and you can take "a couple" of additional questions. If things are going swimmingly, ignore the clock and do this as questions begin to dribble off. After calling for "a couple" of additional questions, take a question, preferably from a reporter you know who has previously been fair to you and your position. If her question is an easy one leading to one of your IMSs, answer it and end the conference with a summary statement, which you should have memorized. If the first question you take after calling for "a couple" more questions is a tough one, answer it, move on, and recognize another reporter—again, someone who's treated you with respect in the past—and take a question from him. I've seen "a couple" of additional questions become three and four as a spokesperson looked for a graceful exit. I don't think this is a good idea. You can wind up ending with a succession of tough queries. If there is no question leading you to one of your IMSs after two questions, end the conference anyway. You don't want to let the news conference run on if it's not going to get positive. Your summary statement should reiterate one of your IMSs so that will be the last thing the assemblage hears regardless of what the last few questions have been.

What if there are no questions after your opening statement? Let's say your advance material and that statement were so thorough that no one has any questions. Either that or the complimentary breakfast you've provided is taking all the media's energy and attention. In this situation, you should prime the pump with a question that puts you on the path to an IMS. Say, "A lot of people ask me . . . ," and ask yourself a question. Or say, "You may be wondering . . . ," and ask yourself a question. Either way, select a question that sets the Q&A session off on a positive footing for you. It can be an easy question that leads directly to an IMS. Or it can be one of the questions from your prepared list of hostile questions—one that you can answer with a deftly built bridge to an IMS. Using one of your tough questions preempts any reporter from asking it. And if a reporter does ask a variation of your tough first question, you can say, "I addressed that in answer to the first question." This same technique is effective if a number of reporters feel compelled to ask you essentially the same question. If you've already answered it, tell them that and move on; there is no need to repeatedly answer the same question.

If there are still no questions from the media after you've asked yourself one or two, just end the conference. Thank everyone for coming, deliver your final summary, and leave the platform.

As with the on-camera demonstration, a news conference begins with you in charge of the agenda. By paying attention to your IMSs and following the few simple rules of conduct for a news conference, you will remain in charge of the agenda throughout the session.

By now you may feel as if you're ready to confront any media opportunity with confidence. But not so fast! Let's take the last chapter to review the basics and determine if you are really ready for *your* fifteen minutes of fame.

CHAPTER 11

GETTING READY FOR YOUR FIFTEEN MINUTES

During the first year of "Good Morning America," the show's talent coordinators managed to get an interview with the legendary actor James Cagney. Cagney, one of Hollywood's original tough-guy gangster actors—and an early song-and-dance man to boot—was then in poor health and lived a reclusive life with his wife on a farm about two hours north of New York City. He had not given an interview in a dozen years or more, so booking him was a real coup. A group of us— David Hartman, two camera crews, a director, and one or two others— drove to his farm one afternoon, and David sat down with the screen legend for about two hours of conversation.

At one point, Hartman asked Cagney the secret of his extraordinarily natural acting style. In his clipped New York Irish accent, Cagney said, "Nothin' to it. Ya walk in, look the other fella in the eye, and tell the truth." I've often felt that with those words Cagney had distilled not only acting but also media interviews. I would argue with him on only the first part of that quote: "Nothin' to it." There is quite a bit to it, both in acting and in media encounters. But if you, as a spokesperson, are prepared as any good actor would be, then it is a lot easier to "look the other fella in the eye and tell the truth."

If you got to this page by reading the previous ten chapters—and not by flipping to the end to see how it all turns out—then you have a good, solid sense of what you need to do before, during, and after you've looked an interviewer in the eye and told the truth. Obey the five commandments of interviews and you will be able to look the other fella in the eye with confidence:

- **Commandment 1: Thou shalt be prepared.** Knowing what you want to say in advance of an interview is the key to preparation. If you do not establish an agenda for each interview you do, you're at the mercy of the reporter's agenda. Even when the reporter's agenda matches your own, you are cheating yourself out of an opportunity to be the most effective spokesperson if you don't prepare a set of messages in advance of the interview. And remember Merlis's Law of Interviews: anyone unprepared for tough questions will be asked tough questions. So if you prepare for the worst and hope for the best, you can't be blindsided in the interview.

- **Commandment 2: Thou shalt know to whom thou art speaking.** You are not talking to the reporter. You are talking through her to her readers, viewers, or listeners. No matter how conversational a reporter is with you, she is working. You should be working, too. Your job is to reach her audience with your intentional message statements. To do that, you speak to them through her.

- **Commandment 3: Thou shalt be quoteworthy.** To effectively communicate your messages, you must express them with economy, with comprehension, and in memorable language. Most good interview subjects for print media or good guests in broadcasting are thought-provoking and accomplished at speaking with a deft ease that appears innate but more often than not is a result of extensive preparation and practice. Use grabbers, or word pictures, that command attention, and speak in soundbites. A good soundbite is a sentence or two or three that captures your audience's attention and delivers a message in a way that's sufficiently dramatic or witty to remain in their memory for a while. Incorporate the sense of an interviewer's question in your answer so your quote or soundbite can stand on its own, needing a minimal introduction or lead-in from the reporter.

- **Commandment 4: Thou shalt practice, practice, practice.** It is not enough to prepare; you must also practice. Read your IMSs out loud to see if they work. Sometimes you won't be able to get your mouth around the phrases you've written; you don't want to find out about that in the middle of a broadcast interview with a microphone recording your every word. The more you practice, the more comfortable you will be with your messages, and the more natural and conversational you'll make them in an interview. Have someone throw questions at you; it's better to hear them coming from another mouth than to ask them of yourself. Record and review your practice sessions.

- **Commandment 5: Thou shalt not lie, evade, nor cop an attitude.** Abraham Lincoln was right when he said, "It is true that you may fool all the people some of the time; you can even fool some of the people all the time; but you can't fool all of the people all the time." Untruths and half-truths have a nasty way of popping to the surface like the insufficiently weighted victim of a mob hit dropped in the ocean. Besides, if you always tell the truth, you won't have to remember what you said. As far as an attitude is concerned, if you alienate the readers, viewers, or listeners, they are going to be negatively disposed to your IMSs.

What to Do Before, During, and After a Media Encounter

In order to follow these five commandments, you will need to take some concrete steps before, during, and after any media encounter. Failure to take all these steps doesn't guarantee doom, but taking them is a virtual guarantee of success.

Before

Determine your agenda for the interview and craft your intentional message statements. When you write them out, keep in mind that your audience is not the reporter, but her readers, viewers, or listeners. Hone your IMSs with grabbers that will make your points linger in the minds of those who hear or read them. And remember, when you are writing your messages and your grabbers, that those readers and listeners are always asking themselves, "Why should I care?" Always incorporate that sensibility into your IMSs.

Make a list of your nightmare questions, and wherever possible, tie one of your IMSs to each of those questions. Study these question-and-answer links: they will be your mental road map from a tough question to an answer that serves your agenda. You can download worksheets for creating IMSs and tough questions at www.master-the-media.com.

Make an effort to check out the reporter's likely agenda. Learn what her publication or broadcast is like. Does it have an agenda or a point of view? How detailed does it get? Does it address a sophisticated or a general audience? What is her style in an interview? There are five questions to ask the reporter who will be interviewing you:

1. What is the direction and thrust of the story?
2. Who else are you interviewing?
3. How much of my time will you need?
4. How long will your article (or broadcast story) run?
5. Do you need or want any documentation, photographs, or videotape?

Before any interview, you'll want to practice responding to challenging questions. Have a colleague or friend aggressively throw questions at you so you can get used to responding with your IMSs; don't quiz yourself, as you're likely to be too gentle. Tape these practice sessions and study your performance.

As close to the interview as possible, check the latest news: watch an all-news cable channel, listen to a radio newscast, or, better yet, check out an Internet news source like the Associated Press's page at http://customwire.ap.org/specials/bluepage.html. Click on any state and then on any publication for access to the wire service's latest, constantly updated news; navigate to the areas in the news you can reasonably be expected to know about and be queried about. You don't want your interviewer to surprise you by asking you about a development you should know about but do not.

If the interview is someplace other than your office or home, arrive at the venue early and establish yourself with the reporter during a preinterview warm-up so she thinks of you as a human being. Use the warm-up to plant the seeds of your IMSs with her; perhaps they'll grow into questions that lead the interview into your agenda.

During

Tape the interview so that you have a record of what you said and how you said it. Also, bring a witness, someone from your organization who knows the subject area of the interview. He'll be available to correct you if you misspeak during the Q&A.

There are four fundamental rules you should adhere to during the interview; they are essential for your success in addressing the reporter's audience—which is your ultimate goal:

1. **Give the headline first and the explanation next.** This is the way the media speak to us—it is also the way we should speak to the media.
2. **Keep it short and simple (KISS).** The longer you make an answer, the more difficult it will be for the reader or listener to absorb.
3. **Activate your jargon filter.** Avoid acronyms and jargon. You and your colleagues will understand what you're saying if you use acronyms and jargon, but the rest of us will be left scratching our heads as we attempt to translate your remarks into English.
4. **Establish your brand.** If it's got a name, use it. It's not "we" or "us," it's the name of your organization. This is critical with the broadcast media, where there is no reread factor.

Remain calm during your interview; your attitude counts even in print interviews, where the reader won't see your face the way a television viewer will. When writing her story, a print media reporter can characterize you as appearing nervous or furtive. If you are prepared with lots of IMSs, you will be calm and resolute.

Don't go off the record or supply information on a not-for-attribution basis or say, "No comment." If you can't answer a question, explain that inability and offer help to the reporter to find her someone who can comment.

During the Q&A, concentrate on your agenda. Since most people have been taught to be polite, it is easy to get sidetracked into the reporter's agenda by dutifully answering her questions. This is fine if her agenda meshes with yours, but that won't always be the case, so keep your IMSs at the forefront of your thoughts and work your answers around to them. Follow these next four steps to move away from her off-the-point or tough questions to get back to your agenda:

1. **Give a short form answer.** You must acknowledge her question or she will ask you again.
2. **Build a bridge.** Just a few words can get you beyond your short form answer and leave you on the threshold of your agenda. Use simple words for your bridges like "on the other hand," "in fact," "however," or "and."
3. **State your IMS.** Move on to one of the points of your agenda. State it at greater length than your short form answer and anchor it with a grabber, a word picture that makes it quoteworthy.
4. **Shut up.** You don't want to add the anticlimactic "And that's why . . ." and restate her off-your-agenda question.

Be specific. The media—and their audiences—love specifics. It is easy to infer the general from the specific, while it is impossible to infer the specific from the general.

An interview is over after the reporter or you leave the premises, not after the notebook, tape recorder, or camera is put away. As long as you are in the presence of a reporter, she is observing and mentally recording. Anything you say in proximity to a reporter or a microphone may be heard by the whole world. A long, long line of world leaders can attest to that fact, including former president Ronald Reagan, former vice president Spiro Agnew, and President George W. Bush, who, as a presidential candidate in 2000, was a little too close to an open microphone when he spotted *New York Times* reporter Adam Clymer and said to running mate Dick Cheney, "There's Adam Clymer—a major-league asshole." To which Cheney replied, also in microphone range, "Oh yeah, big-time."

Watch your words. If there are loaded or negative words in a question, be careful not to repeat them when you are including the sense of the reporter's question in your answer. The "Isn't this a disaster waiting to happen" question is really designed to elicit "This isn't a disaster waiting to happen" from your lips so it can be quoted in print or shown on the air.

After

Offer the reporter the opportunity to fact-check her article or her broadcast script with you; you are not asking for approval rights over what she writes, just offering to check the factual material.

Review your tape of the interview immediately after she leaves. If you discover you misspoke yourself, then call her up and tell her you made a mistake and correct it. If you've omitted a key message point, call her up and tell her that her readers or listeners might want to know about one more point. If you're dissatisfied with your performance, analyze what you did wrong. Every time you listen to that tape, you're learning how to do it right the next time.

Do You Need Professional Media Training?

A lot of companies and individuals offer spokespersons media-training services. One way to tell if you need training is to write up a series of intentional message statements and also some challenging questions. Then have a friend or colleague review "The Interviewer's Top Seven Dirty Tricks" in Chapter 4 and adopt those techniques when he asks you the questions. Videotape the session and look at it to see how successful you were at working your IMSs into the interview. The cosmetics of your response are less important than your ability to work IMSs into the interview. Give yourself a point for every IMS you work into the interview. Deduct one for every IMS on your list that you failed to work into the interview. Did you score zero or less? You probably need training. If you got some, but not all, of your IMSs in, you need to assess how confidently you did it, how well you performed. The bottom line is that only you can answer the question of whether or not you need training by a professional.

If the answer is "yes," you may be tempted to have your in-house public relations person train you. My experience has been that most in-house public relations people don't really want to do it. And with good reason; more often than not, they should not do this sort of training. First, they may not be qualified. Second, if they work for you they may be extremely shy about giving you the proper grilling with tough, make-you-squirm-in-your-seat questions. And, finally, they may also go easy on you when critiquing your performance.

The best advice is to look outside your organization to find a group or an individual that is qualified and trustworthy. The qualified credential is self-evident, but the trustworthy one is equally important because you may be trusting this outsider with intimate and potentially damaging information about you, your business, or your organization. Even if you think that there may not be proprietary information disclosed in training, I can tell you from experience that clients often reveal details they never intended to share during these sessions. So you need to engage the services of a media trainer whose first loyalty is to you as a client, not to the calling of journalism. I was recently summoned to do a media-training session clear across the country because the organization in question didn't trust the person used in the past not to share with his friends in the media some sensational new information the organization was going to announce. Speaking from experience, if a trainer is untrustworthy some of the time, he is untrustworthy all of the time.

Following is a series of questions to ask a prospective trainer:

1. **What are you training me for?** If the first word out of the trainer's mouth is "television," I would find someone else. You need to be trained for media interviews, encounters, and presentations, not just for television. A media trainer who answers with "television" is likely to stress the unique cosmetic considerations of the one-eyed beast over the substance you need to develop for all media. Any coach you engage should customize the curriculum to meet your

needs. For example, if it is highly unlikely you'll ever be ambushed by a TV crew, why waste a valuable chunk of training time with an ambush exercise?

2. **What sort of materials do you leave behind?** Believe it or not, some media trainers don't give you worksheets, a workbook, or other written materials. Others collect the videotape of the interviews when the session ends, which means you can't review your performance at home to learn from your mistakes. More than one client has asked me, "Do you leave behind any materials?" When I asked why they were inquiring, they told me of trainers who took away all workbooks, worksheets, and videotapes, claiming them to be proprietary information. I suppose this action is based on the fear that the internal public relations staff of a company will use the materials to do their own training in the future. As for taking the performance tapes of the individual trainees, I can't fathom the reason for that: a client can't learn from her tape unless she has the tape. Home review of all the media-training materials is an important component of preparation for future interviews. Moreover, those worksheets and videotapes are likely to contain your most feared questions and potentially embarrassing slips of the tongue made during practice interviews. You want that material securely in your own hands, not in the hands of an outsider, even if the outsider has signed a confidentiality agreement. Which brings us to your next question . . .

3. **Do you [the trainer or training organization] have a boiler-plate confidentiality agreement to ensure my organization's secrets will be protected?** Actually, this question should be unnecessary. Any trustworthy trainer should offer you a confidentiality agreement in his initial conversation with you; you should not have to ask about one. Confidentiality should be as high a priority for him as it is for you. Even if your organization has its own confidentiality agreement, I would ask that question in the event the trainer does not offer the information voluntarily. I would caution against even considering any media coach who does not have his own confidentiality agreement or one who tells you that his clients customarily supply an agreement when it's needed. The lack of such a

document indicates insensitivity to the need to protect clients. If you do require your media coach to sign a confidentiality agreement, be certain his camera operator, if he uses one, also signs one.

4. **What is your background?** There is no hard-and-fast rule that someone must have media experience to be a media trainer, but it certainly is easier for the trainer to get inside the head of a reporter if he has been a reporter himself. A lot of media training today is done by former actors and actresses, by public relations and marketing personnel with no direct media experience, and by people whose media experience was at the lowest nonreporting, noninterviewing, nonwriting levels of the mass media. Some of them are very good. But how confident would you be if the pilot of your transatlantic airliner came on the intercom and said, "This is Captain Jones and my background is in aviation. I used to work the check-in counter, and then I was a baggage handler before becoming a pilot. Oh, and this is my fifth flight, so sit back, relax, and enjoy the ride." Ask yourself, "Do I really want someone with no direct, hands-on reporting experience playing reporter in my media training? Do I want someone who specializes in marketing to prepare me for '60 Minutes'-type questions?" Some very large media-training organizations have stables of freelancers who do media training for them. I worked with one once whose stable was filled with thoroughbreds. Former top network producers and reporters were among the cadre. I often thought that if that group had the financial wherewithal, they could run a news-gathering and producing operation that would rival any of the broadcast networks' news operations. Most of these veteran journalists had come to television out of newspapers or newsmagazines, so they had great print backgrounds as well. That sizable and highly qualified group no longer exists today, and in the place of that powerhouse is a cadre of publicists, marketers, and lobbyists, all very experienced—but not in the areas where you want your media trainer to be experienced. You want someone who, in mock interviews, can treat you as a reporter will treat you. Some large public relations firms conduct media training by publicists and bring in a "visiting journalist" to do the interviews. This can prove to be a satisfactory arrangement, although my clients who have done

that tell me it was very costly, and some of them expressed discomfort having an active, working journalist hear their firm's confidential information.

Individual or Group Training

Normally, I prefer groups. For the client, they are highly cost-effective. And even if money is no object, participants in group sessions learn a lot by watching each other—picking up pointers from colleagues' hits and misses. Also, a group is likely to come up with more good intentional message statements, more grabbers, and more tough questions than an individual. One-on-one training can take considerably less time, however—principally because the solo player is the only one who has to be interviewed and critiqued. Solo training is specifically called for when the session is dealing with a unique crisis that only one spokesperson will address or when prepping a spokesperson for a hostile or challenging investigative broadcast interview.

Training is best done away from your personal office, far from the temptation of the phone, fax, and importuning colleagues. A conference room on another floor is good. A hotel meeting room a couple of miles away is even better because there's no way a subordinate or colleague can stroll in to interrupt with some bit of "can't wait" information. Cell phones and pagers should be turned off for the duration of the training session. Actually, turning them off is part of the training because they should be turned off during real interviews, too. I had one client who couldn't turn off his cell phone during training because he was expecting to get word on a big deal at any moment. He spent the better part of the day taking and placing calls and, indeed, concluded the big deal. Unfortunately, he wasn't equipped to announce it to the media. However, he'd brought two colleagues with him, and they stayed with the program and were prepared.

Media training does not end with the close of a session—like any education, it prepares you for further independent study. Sometimes, before a big event or a specific interview, a refresher with a trainer is necessary. It is up to the trainee to keep her IMSs fresh, to come up with new and better grabbers for them, and to do on-camera practice interviews with family or colleagues before embarking on the real thing. It takes some work, but if you're going to be interviewed by the media, making that effort will result in unique opportunities. Not doing the work means you'll be the media's puppet or even victim. Your investment of time and effort will pay dividends in media mastery and reaching through the media to the audience you really want to reach. And remember, when you do reach through the media to readers, viewers, and listeners, you want to be more sensitive to their concerns than the executive in this Dilbert cartoon:

DILBERT reprinted by permission of United Feature Syndicate, Inc.

MEDIA-MASTERING WORKSHEETS

IMS Worksheet 1
Basic Message Points Worksheet

List five intentional message statements you want to work into your next interview.

1. _____

   _____

   _____

   _____

2. _____

   _____

   _____

   _____

3. _____

   _____

   _____

   _____

4. _____

   _____

   _____

   _____

5. _____

   _____

   _____

   _____

IMS WORKSHEET 2
WHY SHOULD I CARE WORKSHEET

Fine-tune your IMSs to answer the public's "Why Should I Care" question. Characterize why they should care about each of your IMSs.

1. _____
   _____
   _____
   _____

2. _____
   _____
   _____
   _____

3. _____
   _____
   _____
   _____

4. _____
   _____
   _____
   _____

5. _____
   _____
   _____
   _____

COMPLETED IMS WORKSHEET 2
WHY SHOULD I CARE WORKSHEET

Fine-tune your IMSs to answer the public's "Why Should I Care"
question. Characterize why they should care about each of your IMSs.
(The WSIC portion is in boldface.)

1. *The nuclear-powered generating plant we want to build outside of Smallville is designed to produce cheap and plentiful power for the next seventy-five years.* **In fact, we project that it will cut consumers' electric bills by 2 to 5 percent a year.**

2. *The plant uses the tried-and-true technology that has been operated safely in the U.S. Navy for more than forty-five years on a total of 467 fighting ships,* **so this extensively-tested and refined technology has an unsurpassed safety record.**

3. *Public safety is our number one concern at Ynot Utilities.* **All of our plant employees will be trained and certified by the U.S. Department of Energy and the state's Occupational and Safety Administration, both of which are totally independent of our company.** *And that training will be constantly updated and refreshed. In fact, every employee will receive forty hours a year of safety training.*

4. *By generating more of our electricity with nuclear-fueled plants, we lessen our reliance on foreign sources of energy and thus make the whole country less dependent on possibly unreliable suppliers and vulnerable supply lines.* **This independence translates to greater physical security of our people and greater fiscal security for our economy.**

5. *France has used nuclear-generating plants for most of its electricity for forty accident-free years.* **This proves that nuclear-fueled electricity can be cheaper and safer when it is based on good science, good engineering, good training, and good oversight. We are committed to supplying all four.**

IMS WORKSHEET 3
GRABBER WORKSHEET

List a grabber for each of your five intentional message statements. A grabber is a word picture that makes your message come alive.

1. _____
   _____
   _____
   _____

2. _____
   _____
   _____
   _____

3. _____
   _____
   _____
   _____

4. _____
   _____
   _____
   _____

5. _____
   _____
   _____
   _____

IMS WORKSHEET 4
WORST QUESTIONS IN THE WORLD WORKSHEET

List your nightmare questions—those you find extremely tough to answer. After each question, write the IMS and grabber you want to use in your answer.

Question: _____

_____

IMS to use in answer: _____

_____

_____

Question: _____

_____

IMS to use in answer: _____

_____

_____

Question: _____

_____

IMS to use in answer: _____

_____

_____

Question: _____

_____

IMS to use in answer: _____

_____